Primp Queen
Fairy Tales

We're Just Like Everyone Else,
Only Prettier

MaryJo Reeves

Originally, this book was written as a birthday present in 2003 for my best friend, Jon.

When she read it she told me I should get it published and I was like "Really?" and she goes "Yeah, totally, you should totally get it published and I was like "Ok!"

This book is intended for entertainment and the beauty advice given should not take the place of your professional beauty advisor.

Everything in this book is true, at least as far as I can remember.

The names have been changed, except for mine and Jon's.

And my Mom's and her Mom's.

Oh and Craig's.

But other than that, they're changed.

Really.

Primp Queen Fairy Tales
We're Just Like Everyone Else...Only Prettier

Published by Orange Soda Publishing (OSP)
Scottsdale, AZ
Copyright © 2016 by MaryJo Reeves
ISBN 978-0-692-78494-5

Edited by Anita Louise Editorial Services LLC

To my Mom, who is a role model, an angel and a complete badass, who taught me that true beauty resides within.

Contents

Introduction

"Oh my God, look at her underwear!" Meri-Lee Henderson shouted from across the girls' locker room.

She was pointing at me, laughing, and gathering a small crowd.

It was the 7th grade, just after P.E. class.

"You have on boys' underpants!" She said.

Then added, "And your legs are all dry and crackly."

I was 12 years old, so of course my mom bought my underwear for me.

I had no say in the matter.

Mom would simply go to Kmart and pick up packages of undies for me, and my three brothers.

Growing up in a household with three prepubescent boys, and being the only girl, I had no idea my underwear should be special or different from theirs.

Until PE class that fateful day.

I did not, in fact, have on boys' underwear, but they were thick and white, with an oversized waistband. Kind of like the girls version of tighty whities.

I was mortified.

Tears welled up in my eyes and my heart made its way to my throat, but I wasn't going to let Meri-Lee Henderson make me cry.

As I was using all of my energy to suck the tears back into my eyeballs, and make an inner vow to always have the most beautiful, gorgeous, silky panties ever made for the rest of my life, a really sweet girl named Jenny Lacy walked over to me.

Jenny was the prettiest girl in our school, and incidentally the nicest.

She was wearing navy blue bra and panty set that looked really expensive and not from Kmart.

Jenny smiled, shrugged her shoulders and said, "There's nothing wrong with your underwear. Do you want to come to my birthday party?"

Jenny is the best, and I mean the very best at diversionary tactics.

"Yes, I'd love to go!" I said with glee and relief.

Then she tossed me a pink bottle of Johnson & Johnson Baby Lotion for my dry and crackly legs.

What's this?

A beauty product? Nice.

I wasn't this excited about a product since my Mom let me use her Jean Nate After Bath Splash and Noxema Cleansing Cream.

Jenny and I immediately forgot all about the boys' underpants, and Meri-Lee Henderson.

I went to Jenny's 12th birthday party the following weekend. It was a sleepover.

There were a handful of girls there.

Meri-Lee Henderson did not make the guest list due to her poor manners.

Each of the girls had changed into different outfits.

I thought it was kind of strange that they would change clothes just to go to a birthday party.

Why not just wear what you wore to school? Right?

No, they changed into outfits, ritzy and clean pressed outfits.

Perfect, persnickety and proper.

One of the girls wore dark, skin-tight Vidal Sassoon jeans, a crisp, double, (possibly triple) starched white button-down shirt with a flouncy red bow at the neck.

And she obviously took the time to completely redo her hair into a sleek, slicked pony tail with a red ribbon that matched her neck-bow.

Jenny wore a very cute baby blue blouse with a tan mini skirt and little blue barrettes in her re-curled, re-styled, re-sprayed hair.

"Do you want to borrow some of my clothes?" Jenny asked, "You know, so you'd feel more comfortable?"

"No thanks. I am comfortable." And then I very politely asked her Mom if I could have two pieces of pizza instead of just one, and she said yes.

I was very concerned that I wouldn't get enough to eat. Much more than if I was wearing an acceptable party outfit.

And anyway, what could be more comfortable than my P.E. tee shirt that was sweat-stained from earlier in the day, and my baggy athletic shorts, tube socks and tennis shoes?

My hair remained in a tangled mess with a pony tail that fell halfway out, halfway through the day.

As it turned out, I was the only one who was able to spend the night.

It was just Jenny and me.

"Did you bring clothes to sleep in?" Jenny asked, concerned.

"Yes," I said, "I'm wearing them."

We stayed up all night talking about our families, fashion, our love and adoration of Jesus, boys (the ones we liked) and what the future might hold.

We talked ourselves into exhaustion.

This was a friendship that would last forever, and somehow we knew it, even then.

I'm not sure when, but at some point she started calling me "Jo" and I called her "Jon."

Those names have stuck with us ever since.

That night, we laughed so hard our tummies ached, and her mom pleaded with us in her deep Kathleen Turner voice "Girls...go to sleep!"

We made a promise to be best friends forever.

No matter what. Pinky swear.

Jon and I would eat lunch together every day, just like all best friends do.

After we'd finished our sandwiches, I'd say "You know what sounds good, an orange soda."

"Yeah!" Jon would say. "That's a great idea!"

From day one, Jon and I were the most agreeable of friends, and honestly, Jon is the best audience that ever lived. She always laughed at every joke or silly comment I made.

One day she looked me dead in the eyes and said "You're the funniest person I ever knew."

Best. Compliment. Ever.

We would get a can of Sunkist Orange Soda, and share it. This went on every day for years and years on end. She always ended up paying for our treat, as I never had any change and she always did.

We figured out that if we counted how much money Jon spent on our post-lunch fizzy beverages, she could have used that money for a down payment on a used Honda Accord.

The syrupy sparkling goodness of the ice-cold orange soda, and the fact that Jon and I shared one every single day for so many years with absolutely no cares of germs or backwash, was in our minds, sweet perfection.

And now, let me tell you about the beautiful,

Wonderfully blissful,

Sometimes a little bit violent friendship that would last a lifetime...

Chapter 1
Sex

"This is terrible news," I said, lying on my bed reading a Cosmo magazine article.

Jon and I were just hanging out in our little dorm room.

"What is it?" Jon replied, sitting at her desk, alternately brushing her thick auburn hair and sipping a diet Pepsi.

I sat up on my bed, and read "The size of a man's penis grows to five inches in circumference when fully erect."

"FIVE INCHES", I repeated in horror.

"That's impossible, do you think that's really true?" Jon gasped as she walked over to see if maybe I read it wrong or simply was making it up to scare her.

While Jon pondered the massiveness of the bomb I had just dropped on her, I collected a ruler, sheet of paper and a pencil.

I began to work on this like an architect with a deadline.

I carefully yet swiftly drew a line five inches long, and made a complete circle. The exhibit was the size of a salad plate.

I'm not kidding. A salad plate.

"No way," Jon said looking at me in fear, her green cat eyes now turning into the size of silver dollars.

Jon and I were both 18-year-old freshmen in college. "No-Sex-until-marriage" was our mantra.

Being Christians, we tried our best to live a life with high moral and ethical standards.

We made it very clear to all of our boyfriends that sex was completely out of the question and non-negotiable.

Jon put it best when she flat-out told one guy "We don't do that," graciously speaking for the both of us.

Because of our forthrightness, we never really had much pressure from guys. They knew exactly what they were in for when they went out with us....a good time.

Sans the sex.

"I must get to the bottom of this," I said stroking on a final coat of Revlon Red nail polish, which, by the way is still considered a cult classic according to several beauty blogs.

"Do we have any reference materials in the room, you know, with pictures?" I asked Jon.

Jon says "Let's see...what if we try looking in our text books?"

"That's a great idea!" I said.

I looked at my books and leafed through the pages.

Nothing in our History Books, English Literature or History of Art.

We didn't even bother opening our math books.

Although we considered it.

I picked up my Introduction to Fashion Merchandising text book, and Jon just shook her head, so I put it down.

We had nothing.

We had no more answers than when we started.

"Maybe we could find someone and ask them."

"But who can we ask?" Jon said quizzically, almost in a panic.

"Maggie!" we both chimed in unison.

Maggie was our R.A. She was beautiful and sophisticated. And she had a hunky, brown-eyed boyfriend named Phil.

I think he was on scholarship for some sport.

And we could tell just by looking at them that they were "doing it."

We never hesitated to go to Maggie for our most concerning issues. We went to her for advice on the latest diet, as she was so slender.

We asked her about the latest beauty products, as she always looked and smelled like she had just taken a shower, shaved her legs and put on a fragrant lotion.

Maggie would have the answer to our burning question. Our dirty, embarrassing sex question, which plagued us to no end.

Jon and I primped for a moment. Just a little hair spray, lip gloss and blush. A touch of mascara and a tiny spritz of perfume.

She chose Anais Anais and I elected for a fragrance by Revlon.

For the life of me I cannot remember the name of the perfume, but I know Revlon made it.

I was a huge fan of Revlon for the simple fact that the factory was in Phoenix. My Mom used to let me shop to my heart's content.

The first time I walked into the factory, at the age of 14, I almost went into shock.

The nice lady behind a giant counter welcomed me and I told her to please hold on while I clutched my chest and caught my breath.

I was stunned by the magnificence.

It was like Charlie and the Chocolate Factory but for cosmetics.

Cases of makeup kits were stacked to the ceiling and each one only cost about $9.00.

There were barrels, drawers and bins filled with lip glosses, nail polishes, eye pencils, mascaras and lipsticks – all for about $1.00.

My wonderful Mom would hand me $100, drop me off and say "Go crazy, kid."

It was a cosmetic wonderland. Oh! And they had all the free samples you could ever fit in your bag.

You could literally take all you want.

When Mom picked me up, I'd thank her and hand her one eye brow pencil.

"Here, Mom, I got this for you," I'd say with a smile.

"Well, how thoughtful," she'd say and we both laughed.

I used to LOVE my Revlon makeup and treasure it.

Norell!

I just thought of the perfume, it was called Norell.

Anyway, Jon and I always primped before leaving the room. You never knew if you might see a cute guy in the hallway.

Jon took a final sip of her diet Pepsi, I grabbed the Cosmo, and off we went.

We knocked on Maggie's door.

No answer.

We knocked again, a little louder this time.

Still nothing. She wasn't home.

"Well," I said, reaching for the doorknob, "Maggie did say her room was always open for us. Let's go in and leave her a note.

I opened the door. The room was dark. Light streamed in from the hallway like an unwelcome intruder, and we heard a gasp and a muffled scream. It was Maggie.

In bed.

With Phil.

Jon and I screamed as loud possible and ran to the safety of our room.

Once we got back to the pristine, virginal, no sex room we called home, we began to laugh hysterically.

A moment later, there was a knock on the door.

"Don't answer it," I said in a low out of breath voice.

Jon ignored my request and slowly opened the door.

"Oh, it's you, come on in."

It was Burt, Jon's boyfriend.

Burt Edwards was a tall, lanky, stylish young media communications student at NAU, who looked strikingly like a young Adam Ant. He could even do the British accent.

Burt wins the award for being the only person to ever make us laugh so hard we'd spew Diet Pepsi though our noses and keel over screaming.

Then we'd get off the floor, and go into a standing ovation, clapping until our hands burned.

Generally, when Burt came to our room, Jon and I would just sit down and prepare to be entertained.

Sometimes he'd put a tape cassette into my stereo and break into a lip-synching dance routine, which looked like he choreographed but turned out he just made it up on the fly.

Jon and I would cheer with delight.

We also thought he was the smartest man alive because he knew about things.

All kinds of things. And he never treated us like we were dumb.

Jon pulled Burt into the room and closed the door behind him, locking it.

"What are you two doing? I thought I heard screaming," Burt said as he sat on the corner of Jon's bed.

"You won't believe what we just saw!" Jon said excitedly.

"Here," I said, interrupting. "Explain this." I thrust the Cosmo into Burt's hands.

Burt looked at the Cosmo and read out loud "Am I a Man Magnet?"

"No, sorry, that's the Cosmo Quiz. Go to the next page," I said.

As Burt read the article that had the mysterious measurement, Jon and I sat in silence, waiting for his explanation.

Burt looked up, saw the ruler, pencil and the drawing on the desk.

"No, you idiots," he said.

Jon and I breathed easier already.

Burt took my pencil, drew 5 inches on a sheet of paper, tore the paper, and folded it up in a round cylinder shaped device.

For just a split second, he looked like a science teacher. He began to explain this enigma to his eager students.

"This is the size. You measured five inches in diameter, not the circumference," he said.

It was the size of a respectable dill pickle.

"Oh," we said "Thank God."

All was well in Allen Hall that night. Until the next morning, when there was a knock on the door.

It was Maggie...

Jon and I always had lots and lots of dates.

Dinner dates, movie dates, double dates, study dates, and church dates even.

We had our calendar prominently displayed.

We had waiting lists and sometimes double booked just for the thrill of it.

We even decided to make a game out of it.

One week we only dated guys with blond hair.

Another week it was just guys with hot cars.

One time a really cute guy asked me out. "Not this week," I said, "But next week I will be exclusively dating Engineering majors."

There was "guys in uniforms week." And then we had "brown eyes week."

We even decided to spice it up further by incorporating a little friendly competition. It was "Only date guys with the same first initial week."

I thought I had beaten Jon with my two Tony's, which should have counted double word score because they not only have the first initial, they had the same name, but she brutally defeated me with her three Dave's, a Don and a Dan.

Impressive.

Jon had a dilemma arise one day, when her long distance, long-term boyfriend, Christian was coming for a visit.

Poor Christian.

He thought things were going great with the dramatic, serious and lengthy phone conversations with Jon that bored me to tears.

Jon would look at me and mouth the words "Help me" and I would point to my watch and silently try to tell her we were running late for our double date.

Christian came to visit Jon and stayed with us for a couple of days and let me tell you, my job was grueling. I had to answer the phone for both Jon and my own date requests.

The hardest part was trying to figure out how to take messages for Jon's dates without Christian finding out she was dating other guys.

At first Jon felt guilty, but I told her she didn't sign any contracts and could date whomever she pleased.

She was like, right, right, no contract.

I would answer the phone, grab my clipboard and slither into the hallway.

Then Jon would yell out to me, "If that's Lola, tell her YES, I do want to have lunch with her next week for sure. Tell her yes. Did you tell her yes?

Lola was one of Jon's "Dave's" We had given them code names.

We had to. It was the only way to keep them straight and not have mishaps.

"Yep, you are having lunch with Lola on Tuesday," I said, putting my pen behind my ear.

Then I added "And on Wednesday we're going to the movies with Franchesca and Penelope." (code names for Frank and Patrick).

"Sounds good," Jon said and winked.

Jon and Christian began dating during our junior year in high school.

Upon graduation, they decided have a long distance relationship while Jon went to away to college with me, and Christian moved to California to work.

Years prior, Christian started out as my boyfriend our freshman year in high school.

The first time I saw him, I was literally rendered speechless.

Jon and I were so excited to finally be in high school.

My mom let me start wearing makeup.

I had grown a couple of inches taller that summer and both filled out and slimmed down in all the right places if you know what I mean.

While all of us girls on the volleyball team were stretching out, I saw a boy on a ten-speed bike, wearing a white tee shirt and white shorts.

I stared in awe as he rode passed the volleyball courts.

Was this a mirage?

Was I imagining this beautiful vision in white on a Schwinn?

There he goes, I thought.

Will I ever see him again?

He was perfect. Absolutely perfect.

I must meet him.

A few days later, school started. And there he was.

The new boy.

The new boy with green eyes and a kind, sweet smile that would melt your heart.

And he smelled really fresh and was super athletic.

The problem: there was only one of him and many, many girls.

And all the girls liked Christian.

All of them.

Girls with double pierced ears, perfectly feathered hair, designer clothes and trust funds.

Slutty pastors' daughters.

I was no match.

Thinking fast, I decided that I needed to get his attention.

I didn't want to be overly flirtatious or extra loud.

No. I had to do something different.

Something the other girls didn't think of.

I wasn't sure what to do, or how to do it.

In between classes, I'd follow him, and one day, I followed too closely and inadvertently stepped on the back of his shoe.

And he noticed me as a result.

So I kept doing that.

It seemed like a good idea.

He would turn around and look really annoyed.

"Oh, sorry...I didn't see you... I thought you were someone...have we met?" I'd say.

"Did you step on his tennis shoes again after Algebra?" Jon would ask excitedly.

"Yep!" I said, "He either really likes me, or really hates me, I can't tell."

This idea actually worked!

After stepping on his Nike's enough times and watching him kneel down, put it back on, re-tie it and shake his head and walk away, he finally saw something in me.

He asked me to Homecoming.

Me! This was the equivalent to Cinderella being asked to the ball.

This was fantastic news.

The gown shopping, shoe shopping, evening bag shopping.

I had work to do.

Christian himself told me that I wasn't the prettiest girl in school, but I was the most persistent.

I'll take it.

We spent all year being boyfriend and girlfriend. We held hands. Shared some inside jokes. Went out for ice cream. He walked me home from school every day and even carried my books.

He was darling.

It was really great at first, then it got a little, well, let's just say Christian had some emotional issues.

He was very sensitive, which is nice at first because it manifested in poetry, perfume and soft cuddly teddy bears as gifts.

But then you might hear a conversation that went a little like this:

"Hey guys, where's Christian?" someone would say.

"He's in the bathroom...crying," someone would answer.

"Oh, Right," the other person would say.

Even though this was a bit draining, I was devastated when he broke up with me.

Well, he tried to break up with me.

It came in the form of a phone call.

"I really like you, but we're so young, I think we should go out with other people," he says to me.

Over the *phone*.

"Christian, what are you trying to say?" I asked.

"I'm breaking up with you."

"I don't understand. Can you please say it again, only slower and maybe louder?"

"I'm breaking up with you, I'm sorry" he said again, softly with the sweetest most apologetic tone I ever heard.

That's the thing about Christian, he was always so darn nice.

Nevertheless, after we hung up I waited for him to show up for our date.

He never said he was canceling for tonight...he just said something about friendship and blah blah.

It got dark out.

I waited.

What could be keeping him?

I re-curled my hair. Feathered. Sprayed. Flip.

Sprayed. Sprayed.

I waited some more.

I changed my earrings. The ones I had in were all wrong.

Waiting.

Seriously what was keeping him?

I applied more lip-gloss.

I watched the first half of Saturday Night Live.

Musical Guest: The Fixx performing "One Thing Leads to Another."

And I waited.

My Mom walked in my room and said "I don't think he's coming over."

He didn't come over.

Ever again.

The radio didn't help:

"Turn around, every now and then I get a
little bit lonely and you're never coming 'round
Turn around, Every now and then I get a
little bit tired of listening to the sound of my tears."

I really was tired of listening to the sound of my tears.

I think Bonnie Tyler summed it up the best because it seriously was a total eclipse of the heart.

The next morning, I called Jon.

When she answered the phone, I couldn't speak. I just wailed.

I cried so hard it actually hurt my throat.

She simply said two words.

"Come over."

She greeted me at the door saying, "The toothpaste is in the medicine cabinet."

But then she sees that I held up my toothbrush and a tube of Pepsodent as I walked right passed her.

Jon knows when I am really, *really* upset I have to brush my teeth. First thing.

She took care of me all day and we talked all night until the next morning.

Jon always knew how to make everything better.

"It's going to be ok, I promise," Jon said and hugged me.

"Hey, do you want pancakes? Let's have pancakes!" Jon proposed.

"That's a great idea!"

Then we went into her kitchen and she goes "Do you know how to make pancakes?"

Jon's sister, Paige heard the commotion and walked by saying something under her breathe like "What a couple of idiots."

And we were like "Paige! Do you know how to make pancakes!?"

She didn't answer.

"Paige?"

"Paige?"

She must not have heard us.

Thankfully her Mom was there and made them for us.

The next week at school, I found out the gruesome, disturbing, almost debilitating news that Christian dumped me for Traci Ferberger.

Traci Ferberger was an adorable cheerleader who I found truly revolting in every way.

And yes, she dotted her "i" with a heart.

She was from Texas and played the country-girl-damsel-in-distress for all it was worth.

"Oh my goodness, look at that, I dropped my pencil, I do declare," she would say with her southern drawl and five guys would swarm over to pick it up for her.

I was so despondent my weight plummeted to 89 pounds.

I had to safety pin the waist of my Levi's 501 button up jeans so they didn't fall off me.

I also got a pixie haircut, partly because I was depressed and partly because I wanted to look like Olivia Newton John in her "Let's Get Physical" video.

Unfortunately, I looked nothing like Olivia Newton John, so I had to wear really big earrings so I wasn't mistaken for a 12 year-old boy.

Shortly after Christian and Traci Ferberger broke up, he very briefly dated our friend Kate, then began a serious relationship with Jon.

By the time he and Jon started dating, my hair had grown out and I began dating Danny Perez.

Danny Perez was an extremely good looking, studious track star who smelled as fresh as a spring day and only lived to hear my stories.

His personal hygiene was second to none.

He got a haircut every 6 weeks without exception, and his skin was 100% blemish-free.

Breath: minty fresh at all times.

He ate three meals a day.

No snacking in between and I can't say for sure, but I would bet dollars to donuts he flossed daily.

He ironed his jeans. I'm not kidding, he actually ironed his jeans.

Everything he did was correct and proper and nothing was out of order in his car, on his person or in his home at any time, for any reason.

I met Danny in the middle of my sophomore year in high school.

A mutual friend introduced us. He walked up to me, and we said hello.

Just minutes before this meet and greet, I learned he'd just crashed on a motorbike.

Danny was ok but his friend was injured.

Danny and I talked for a moment, and I said, "Do you think your friend needs to go to the hospital?"

"You know because he's bleeding from the head?" I added.

"Oh, right, yeah....um can I call you?" he says to me.

Danny was my first actual real love.

We dated for about two years.

And we would make out until our lips were bleeding.

Bleeding, I tell you.

He was also all about the manners, protocol, and procedures and was concerned about class and elegance.

One year at the prom, I was still hungry after the dinner and told Danny.

Just letting him know I would like to go to Wendy's later that night for a single with pickles and ketchup.

Normally Danny would be delighted to take me to Wendy's for a single with pickles and ketchup, but I said this *during* the dinner and other kids heard me, which I really didn't care, but Danny did.

He shushed me.

He actually *shushed* me.

Like this "Shhhh!"

I felt like that video by Til Tuesday "Voices Carry," where the guy is saying hush hush.

But it wasn't about my being the other woman, it was about the ridiculously tiny portion at this so-called "dinner."

I think the shushing was an involuntary response, because even he looked surprised after he did it.

"Oh, sorry, darling," I said.

I then blotted the corner of my mouth with my napkin, placed it gently on my lap, like a lady, and leaned over to his friend and said "Hi, excuse me, are you going to eat that potato?"

Danny put his head down as if he was defeated and apologized to his friend for my behavior.

Then I said to his friend "Seriously, if you don't have any big plans for that potato, would you mind passing it down here?"

His friend passed me his potato and I was like "Oh, and the butter, thank you."

I loved to make Danny uncomfortable every now and then, and I believe he found me whimsical, charming and delightful.

Most of the time.

We had a lot of wonderful times together. But I knew he wasn't the one for me.

The breakup was heart wrenching for both of us, but as we stayed together, things started to change for the worse. And finally our relationship was on life support.

I pulled the plug.

I loved him, really and truly, but I knew if I didn't end it in a timely manner, things were just going to get more serious and I'd end up married to a really nice man, but not Mr. Right.

Although, don't think for a moment that I didn't daydream about the alternate ending for my life story.

Danny and I would have both gone to ASU.

He would've joined a frat and I would've been a sorority girl.

We'd graduate college, have a huge wedding where my color scheme would have been peach and yellow.

I know! Peach and yellow sounds terrible, but remember this was the 80's.

And it's my *alternate* ending.

Not what really happened.

We would have two daughters: Britney Pamela and Victoria Adrianna.

I would have dressed them in identical outfits at all times.

And then oops! Little Vanessa Cassandra would have been our third baby and a total surprise but that's ok because we kept all of Victoria Adrianna's baby clothes.

We would have a little fluffy dog with a bejeweled collar named "Jacqueline Bouvier Kennedy Onassis," and a gold fish named "Madonna."

Or, my secondary alternate ending is where we only have one child, a son, and we name him James.

Danny's mother would make me promise to use "Robert" for his middle name because that's Danny's middle name.

Although James Robert is very nice name, I would change the middle name to "Louis" because that's my Grandfather's name.

And instead of a dog, we'd have a cat named "Graham Crackers."

That was not how my life was supposed to go and I knew it. I just knew it deep down.

That didn't make it any easier, though. It still hurt me deeply that we were no longer together.

I cried for weeks. I wanted to call him every single day and I had to stop myself. I couldn't mess with his head or play games. I had to make a clean break.

All day long I would think to myself that I don't have him anymore and I never will again.

I mourned the loss of that relationship. Deeply.

"Do you think it's time to take down the pictures?" My Mom asked me.

I kept our prom and homecoming pictures up in my room for several weeks.

My mom gave me a three-week grace period and then strongly encouraged me to take the pictures down.

The only thing that helped was going out with other boys. Lots and lots of boys!

Meanwhile, Jon and Christian were becoming quite serious. Things were just humming along for them. Everything seemed fabulous.

One other thing about Christian and his sensitivity that drove me batty is he was hands down then most romantic person who ever lived.

He was a walking Billy Ocean song.

His romantic endeavors knew no end. He was all about the romance and the pageantry of it all.

He actually took singing lessons and a song writing class so he could sing to his future bride at their wedding.

Nope, not making it up.

He came out to visit Jon, with full intention of proposing marriage.

She was having the time of her life and he was going to put an end to it.

Jon didn't know about the looming proposal, but somehow, strangely enough, I did.

"I know something's going on," Jon says to me. "What is it? You have to tell me. You have to." She insisted.

I told her she was going to either receive a package in the mail or a person was going to visit.

We giggled about it for several days, and then, one day Jon got serious.

"Listen," she says. "I need you to tell me if Christian is coming here."

She looked like she was going to cry.

"If Christian comes out here, I think he's going to ask me to marry him." She says.

"And I can't marry him," Jon's eyes filled with tears.

I went to our mini-fridge and took out two cans of beer.

Jon and I didn't usually drink, but I think this was a time-and-place sort of situation.

I was under no circumstances to tell Jon about his intentions to propose.

Sworn to secrecy.

I was to tell No One.

Luckily, I could not be trusted with this information.

We drank our beers and I spilled the details.

"Yes, he's coming out here to see you." I said

"He is going to propose to you."

"He is," I say after taking a sip of beer and motioning for her to do the same.

"Oh my God. I can't do it. I can't. What am I going to do?" she said.

It was too late to cancel. Christian showed up the next day.

He brought gifts.

I swear this is true, may my highlights turn brassy if I'm lying:

He brought Jon matching "his and hers sweatshirts" for them to wear.

The matching sweatshirts had a picture of two teddy bears riding a tandem bicycle, and the bears had matching sweatshirts on, too.

Christian thought that was a great idea.

"Where's your sweatshirt?" he'd ask, all smiling.

"Go put your sweatshirt on, Silly!" He'd say and tickle Jon then hug her.

I put my hand on Jon's shoulder and gave her my deepest, most heartfelt of condolences, "I'm so sorry."

After a few days of gathering her thoughts, Jon cleared her head from the Christian Fog.

Jon was finished.

Christian was not her Mr. Right and she knew it.

"Look what else he brought me, Jo."

I walked over, and opened a light brown box.

Inside was a necklace he obviously got in Flagstaff. "For the love of God, is that a beaded necklace?" I gasped.

Jon didn't answer, she simply held up the matching earrings and we both started laughing.

Turquoise! Sweet mother of all that is pure and holy, was he deluded, thinking she would be caught dead in that?

I know this kind of jewelry is all the rage now, and I have even considered incorporating turquoise into my wardrobe of jewels, but two things:

1. Jon was very particular about accessories
2. These were not something either of us found attractive in the 80's

Previous gifts included, but were not limited to: the music box. Not just any music box.

This one was hand crafted by Christian himself.

When you open it up, it played "My Favorite Things."

On top of the box, was a heart shaped cookie Jon had previously baked for Christian.

He saved the cookie, lacquered it up and securely glued it on top of the box.

On top of the cookie was a single dried out rose from a bouquet of roses Christian gave her for some other occasion, sealed with a lacquer.

The time had come for the break up.

Jon and I went to Phoenix and spent the weekend at my parents' house, which was a ritual we observed so I could go to my orthodontist to get my braces tightened each month.

So painful.

But after my appointment, Jon would take me to Dairy Queen and we'd get Snickers Blizzards simply because I liked the challenge of trying to get frozen caramel out of the metal in my teeth.

And those Blizzards were so darn good.

Anyway, Jon was in a bind because she had to break up with Christian and I had no experience with something so serious and grown up.

Jon looked at me so deeply and seriously and said "I *really* need my Mom right now."

Her mom was very sick at the time, living in another state no less.

"I know you need your mom, but since she's not here, you can use mine." I said as if offering her a handbag I still used, and got a lot of compliments on over the years so I would definitely want it back.

Then I stuck my finger in my mouth to dig out remnants of Snickers caught in the far back of my braces.

Just then, my Mom walked into the bedroom and said "Jenny, if you need to talk, I'm here."

My Mom is awesome at giving advice and pointing out exactly the reality of situations.

She can help you see the truth, the reality, and then she empowers you to make up your mind and really stick to your guns.

Mom always taught me it's good to get advice, but always make up your own mind.

She also makes the CIA look silly when it comes to surveillance, and was a ninja eavesdropper.

She didn't care who knew it, either.

It wasn't something she tried to hide or pretend it wasn't happening.

She saw all. She knew all. Nothing got passed my Mom.

She was never caught "cleaning" your room and "happened upon" your personal belongings.

No. Trust me.

If you lived in my parents' house, my Mom went through your stuff.

Jon and my Mom talked for a long time.

My Mom then handed Jon the phone.

"It's ok honey, you need to do this."

I don't know how long she was on the phone breaking up with Christian, because I was busy preparing for the evening.

I wanted to help, so I did my part. I got on the phone with one of my boyfriends and "ordered" a date for Jon. Andy was a Phoenix-based boyfriend I had.

I met Andy on my high school graduation day, which happily fell on my 18th birthday.

Someone had a huge house-party with tons of people that night.

A limo pulled up and everyone looked over as leggy bleach blonde Noelle Nash piled out in sky-high crimson heels, and a cherry-red, skin-tight mini dress.

Noelle Nash always looked super-hot.

Noelle immediately spotted me and handed me a half-empty bottle of champagne and dramatically air kissed me on both cheeks.

And she brought goodies:

Three guys exited the limo who looked like Abercrombie and Fitch models.

"Ewww! I want one! I want one!" I yelped.

"Go ahead, Doll, take your pick," Noelle said in slurred speech as she plowed passed me to greet the other party-goers.

"You. Come dance with me," I demanded while pointing to the cutest one.

And that's how I met Andy.

He was slim and tan, with chiseled cheekbones and rock hard abs.

His eyes were bluer than a Blue Raspberry Slurpie from Seven Eleven and he dressed like Duran Duran.

And he drove a very fast and adorable sports car.

"Hi, Andy, I need a date for my friend Jenny. She just broke up with her boyfriend and she needs to go out and have some fun tonight, let's double." I proposed while chomping bubble gum and curling my hair.

Andy pulled through with "Jim," another Abercrombie guy with a mischievous grin, who also dressed like Duran Duran.

Jon came back into my bedroom after the break-up phone call took place.

She plopped on my bed and looked exhausted from crying.

She didn't say anything for a long time. We just sat there.

"I ruined his life."

"Ruined."

Then she added, "He thought we were going to get married. He wrote a song...." She went on.

I needed to get her mind off this mess.

I tossed her a mini skirt and an eye shadow pallet and told her to get dressed for her date tonight.

I expected Jon to decline, seeing as how she just destroyed Christian's life forever.

Instead, she begins primping and asks me "Did you tell him I have green eyes and long legs?"

"Yes," I said, completely impressed with her resilience.

We went out that night, with our Duran Duran boys, and had a blast.

Over the years Christian's name came up here and there.

He ended up marrying a girl named Jenny.

We thought it was a coincidence, until we heard he was divorced years later.

Only to find and marry another girl named Jenny. Weird.

Early one chilly morning at NAU, Jon and I went to visit our friend, Kara.

She lived on the second floor in Allen Hall. We walked in, and Kara was peering out the window.

"You won't believe this. Look."

We looked down and someone had stomped words into the snow in enormous letters:

KARA, MOVIE TONIGHT?

Then, upon closer inspection we saw August Fiscus, a fellow NAU student. He stood there, with his arms open, looking up at Kara with love and adoration.

Romantic.

"I can't go out with him, I'm too busy," Kara whispered to us.

I grabbed her by the shoulders and said, "Yes, you're going out with him, Kara."

"You have to go, Kara," Jon said, opening her closet and picking out an outfit she should wear on the date.

"And you have to wear something super, *super* cute!" she added.

This act of romance even rivaled Christian's music box.

Jon and I were both suckers for a guy that put himself through physical pain just to show his infatuation.

Jon rested her chin in her hands, and elbows on the windowsill, looking at the message.

"He must have been up all night treading through the snow."

I peeked over Jon's head to also admire the work, and to very briefly wonder why August Fiscus liked Kara and not me.

What was that all about?

I said, "That's so romantic. Hey, Jon, remember Monty used to go out of his way to find out what Christian gave you as a gift and then go out and buy you a larger, better version of whatever it was?"

"Yeah," Jon smiled, tilting her head the way she did when she thought about a guy she really liked.

Jon said to me "Remember that one guy who sent you dozens and dozens of pink and yellow roses?"

"Oh yeah, I met him at a stoplight," I beamed.

Then I said, "Remember that guy who burned your house down to get your attention?"

No, that was "Endless Love," she said.

"Oh yeah, totally good movie..." we both agreed.

The Phoenix summer was alive with all kinds of promise, hope and possibilities.

My Drill Sergeant took me my very first college party in June 1986.

My brother John is three years older than me, and was more like an authority figure than a sibling. Although I do love him dearly.

He was a commissioned officer in the Army and served many years in the Arizona National Guard, so I just refer to him as My Drill Sergeant, because he would often raise his voice, express disapproval and command me to study more and party less.

"Sir, yes sir!" I'd say after he'd call to check on me.

Often I'd run into him on campus and he would be in his official Army uniform and reprimand me like I was a recruit.

"Say it, don't spray it," I'd say.

He didn't think that was funny at all, by the way.

Anyway, My Drill Sergeant kindly took me to my first college party.

We show up at the house party and there's someone standing in the kitchen.

He notices me.

I think he looks familiar so I smile and kind of half-wave, then stop once I realize I don't know him.

He walks over and introduces himself.

Rob Carter.

Seems like a nice guy.

Cute guy.

College Guy – and I was just barely out of high-school, so this was uncharted territory.

We talk for a bit, then he says to me "I'm taking you out next Saturday night."

"No thanks," I say, sipping my rum and coke.

I look around the room.

People are slamming tequila shooters.

Whitesnake is blaring on the radio.

"Here I go again on my own.
Going down the only road I've ever known..."

There's laughter and things are spilled on the carpet.

Someone's parents are going to be really mad, I thought.

Rob Carter then took my hand, smiled and said "I'm definitely taking you out Saturday night."

"Um, no thank you," I say, but cannot stop smiling.

He was so persistent and so cute, I found myself saying yes.

Twirling my hair with my finger and saying yes.

Now keep in mind he is my Drill Sergeant's Delta Chi Frat brother, so I asked his opinion on the matter.

Everyone thinks because I have three brothers that they were overly protective but the truth is they pretty much stayed out of my love life.

But I truly valued my Drill Sergeant's input.

I trusted him.

And here's how that conversation went.

"What do you think of Rob?"

"Not a good idea."

"I think he's cute."

"I'd stay away."

"I like him," I said looking over my Drill Sergeant's shoulder to get a better look at Rob.

"You can do what you want, but I strongly advise against it."

"He's hot"

"Again, not a good idea"

"Such a cute smile"

"I'd move on if I were you."

"And he's seems really nice…."

"You'll regret it."

And that was that.

Case closed.

I went out with Rob the following weekend.

Rob rode a motorcycle and wore a miniature diamond earring stud. Which by the way, he ending up giving to me. I treasured it.

I figured if he gave me his diamond earring, I was the only girl he liked.

Right?

I did téll him he had to remove the earring before he came to the door to pick me up because my Dad wouldn't like it.

And he obliged. He showed up. No earring.

He knocked on the door, I answered it, he said a quick hello to my Mom and Dad and off we went.

When I got home that night just before my 11pm curfew, my Dad goes "By the way, I saw the pierced ear."

Then my Dad goes "Why does that boy have an earring?"

Rob was an all American Boy, with this bad-boy side one could not ignore.

He was ridiculously smart and could pretty much charm the panties right off you.

He always had a look on his face like he knew a really juicy secret, or was about to tell a really dirty joke.

I really began to like Rob a lot.

I liked his attitude and his confidence. He made me laugh all the time.

He would pick me up on his motorcycle and off we'd go.

I didn't care where we went as long as I was holding on tight, resting my head on his back, my long hair flowing.

And honestly, I must say, he was the best kisser ever.

You simply just have not lived unless you were kissed by Rob Carter.

Jon hated Rob Carter with an intense burning passion for no other reason than the fact that I liked him more than he liked me.

Her loathing was based on this technicality, and he could never, ever be redeemed.

"You know he goes out with other girls," she warned.

"No he's doesn't, he gave *me* his earring, see?" I said as I tucked my hair behind my ear.

I'd sit and wait for Rob to call.

"He's going to call."

"Any minute now."

I'd wait for the phone to ring.

One day I went back to our dorm room and told Jon about a homework assignment I got in my Human Relations class. We were supposed to write down our life dream.

What did we want our life to be 5, 10, 20 years from now. What did we want out of life.

I sat on my bed and excitedly handed Jon my paper.

Jon holds the paper, smiles at me with pride, settles on the bed, clears her throat and reads the assignment, looking like a mom admiring her child's work.

She read it quietly. Her face fell from a proud smile to a look of disgust.

She turns the paper over to see if she was missing something.

"That's it?" she says.

"That's your big dream for your whole life?" she says, with disdain.

"Your big life dream is to *marry Rob*?" she said with venom in her voice.

She tossed the paper on the desk and puts her hands out like "Please, come on."

"What is wrong with you, oh my God, that's your big life dream – to marry ROB?"

"No," I say slowly.

"We'd have kids, too."

I had it all planned.

We'd get on his motorcycle and ride to Vermont and live in an old farmhouse and live on love and he'd tell me I'm pretty.

And there would be butterflies and rainbows.

Jon was horrified.

"I think you really need to get a clue, MaryJo," she said.

The truth is, I really thought that's what I wanted.

Rob was one of those guys who was so smart and charming, that I could hardly speak when he was around.

I'd get tongue-tied and all giddy even when someone mentioned his name.

He made me feel so many things.

"You seriously lose IQ points when he's with you, Jo," Jon said.

Then she added, "Seriously."

The truth is, I really didn't know this boy but I had feelings for him.

It was a huge crush.

My boy craziness knew no bounds.

"You know," Jon said, "I think the reason you like him so much is because he's not into you."

Then she went on to say "The minute a guy falls for you, you forget all about them."

"You literally forget about them. Like someone has to remind you who they are."

"What!" I exclaimed, "That's not true, name one."

"Keith Armstrong," She said.

"Oh, well, yeah..." I said.

Then she added "Matt Kosowski, David Dunn, Tim Hodges, Gary Stevenson, the Fitzimmen brothers, Mark Thomas, Steve Thomas (no relation), and the cross country team in the class of '84."

"The Cross Country Team of 1984 really did love me," I said.

Maybe Jon was right. Maybe I wouldn't have been so hung up on Rob if he had been in love with me.

Anyway, my romance with Rob fizzled out quickly. I was glad I met him, but I knew we were never meant to be.

Rob was gone with the new semester.

Maybe he went to Vermont and got a farmhouse without me.

Someone who knew someone who knew his friend Corbin said Rob joined the Navy.

Oh well, there will always be more boys...

Chapter 2
Food

Jon and I enjoyed our junk food, for sure. Especially chocolate.

And anything with sprinkles.

Also, anything fried, cream filled, hand dipped, frosted or sugarcoated. Or anything you'd dunk in milk.

One might wonder how we managed to maintain our cute little figures, but the truth is we usually only ate once a day.

We also burned massive calories because we ran, skipped, jogged and galloped everywhere. All the time.

If Jon and I were ever the lucky recipients of food-gifts, we would often forego all other foods and just live on the food-gift, then resume eating normally again.

Jon's stepmom, Luvie, once sent us a fifteen-pound bag of trail mix from Costco, which we lived on almost exclusively for several days on end.

We sat in the middle of the floor facing each other and ate only the chocolate pieces.

"Ok, Jon said, "Try putting an almond in your mouth with two chocolate pieces and you'll swear you're eating a Hershey's Bar with almonds.

"That's a great idea!"

We consumed the entire bag and threw away five pounds of leftover raisins, cashews and dried apricots without a hint of regret.

This was not unlike the time NAU advertised to our parents the option of sending small, medium or large fruit baskets to their kids kind of like a

Welcome-to-College-Now-Eat-Your-Fruit-Basket.

Jon's Mom, my Mom, my Aunt Mary, and my Gram each sent us the largest fruit basket option. Of course. Nothing but the best. All wrapped up pretty with bows and cellophane.

Again, simply because it was there, we only ate fruit. Just fruit and fruit only.

I loved it! I was never so regular in my whole life.

We loved our food-gifts.

Usually around Valentine's Day Jon and I would have a collection of chocolate boxes that made our dorm look like a See's Candy franchise.

We would receive boxes and boxes of chocolate truffles, nougats, and caramels, with and without nuts.

We'd donate the flowers to our friends in the dorm. But we kept the candy.

Jon and I had an agreement to share each piece of chocolate.

She would take a bite of one of the chocolates, tell me know exactly what was in it and how it tasted, and I would decide if I wanted the other half.

And vice versa.

So, it was normal to see a box of chocolates with one or two candies that had been bitten into.

Other people were very grossed out by this, by the way.

And that was fine because we were not really into sharing with outsiders.

Once during a boy-related crisis, most likely Rob Carter-related, I went home and took a bite out of each and every candy.

I closed the boxes and put them back on our little snack cart.

Jon came home from her class, and decided she'd like a piece of candy.

She opened one box, saw the mess of half eaten candies.

Not one candy in any of the boxes had been left intact.

"Oh, honey, what's *wrong*?"

She knew how sensitive I was to heartbreak. I cried and told her all about it. She totally got it, as she always does.

One time we got a package from my Grandmother.

Gram made Italian cookies, which were so thick and heavy, they were more like dense bread.

The box was the size of a large kitchen appliance and it took two frat guys to lug it up three flights of stairs to our room.

"Hey! This box is full of Gram's Cookies!" One of the guys shouted."

Jon and I told them to just keep walking.

Nothing to see here.

Every person who knew Gram, or knew someone who knew Gram experienced her wonderful homemade cookies.

Gram was like my second mom, taught me many things from the time I was a baby until adulthood. She taught me how to drink out of a cup, how to sew a button, and how to get a house really, *really* clean.

She was there when I had a broken heart by a boy, when Jon and I had a fight, when my parents were working full time, all the time.

One of my fondest memories of Gram is when I was little, we'd scour the house clean to perfection, then go to the store and buy ingredients for cookies and fudge and bake all afternoon.

The smell of bleach and baked goods permeated the air.

Heaven.

And my Gram had the best laugh. You would want to tell her stories just to hear her musical laughter.

Then when I'd go home from college for the weekend or holidays, she'd say "Come on Princess, let's have a snack."

We would sit at the kitchen table drinking wine and eating bread dipped in olive oil.

Jon and I were now the proud owners of our own stash of Gram's cookies.

When the girls in the dorm got curious about our huge box of cookies and wanted to know what was in it, we just told them we got a kitten.

Again, not that into sharing.

I am not proud of this, but Jon and I ate nothing and I mean nothing but Gram's cookies for one solid month.

Jon and I never spoke about the fact that we sustained our lives on Gram's cookies for over thirty days.

After the last crumb was eaten, we stood over the empty box looking in to double-check for leftover crumbs.

I looked up at Jon. We were both very sad.

"They're gone. All Gram's cookies are gone."

Then we resumed eating normal food again.

This was disgusting even for us and we knew it. So, we never told anyone.

We were not above stealing junk food, either.

Debbie and Debbie lived across the hall from us.

"Jon," I said walking into the room and putting my books on the desk.

"The Debbie's have m&ms....let's go get some."

"Just walk over and take their candy?" Jon asked, adding "But they don't even like us, especially you."

"And won't they see us, you know, if we just walk in their room and take their candy? Wouldn't that get awkward, like, really fast?

"Right, but let's just go over and say hi, and act like it's a friendly visit." I said, smiling.

Jon pondered, "Are they peanut?"

"Yes," I said.

"Are they the new pastel Easter colors?" Jon asked.

"Yep!" I said.

The candy not only had to taste good, it also had to be really pretty.

So we walked over, knocked on their door and were quite friendly asking about how their day was and "Oh, look, m&m's."

I think they appreciated the visit and were happy to share their candy with us.

In our second semester Jon got a part time job.

She had a full class load, too, so she seemed to always be in a rush.

I wanted to help her out, so I'd fix little meals for us both.

I just made simple little things like yogurt with granola, grilled cheese sandwiches, Campbell's tomato soup. Stuff like that.

Easy peasy.

Jon was very grateful.

One day she came back into the room holding her tummy with both hands.

"Something's wrong with me," she said.

Then she went on, "I had to leave my class like four times to use the bathroom."

"Oh, really?" I said, "That's weird, do you have the flu, or what?"

"No, I just keep having to go to the bathroom all the time lately."

"Oh!" I said, jumping up and going to the fridge. "Maybe it's because of this."

I held up a large jar of unprocessed bran.

"I've been adding heaping tablespoons full of this to everything we eat. Isn't it great?"

"What? Why did you do that? Are you trying to kill me?" Jon asked.

Then she added a very hurtful "Not everyone's constipated like you are, MaryJo."

This is what earned me the nickname "The Bran Fairy."

After that Jon either fixed her own food, or went to the dining hall to eat.

Without me.

One Saturday evening Jon and I were just hanging out in our little dorm room.

We decided we'd like a snack. It was chilly and rainy out, perfect for just staying in and watching a movie.

Tonight, we wanted to be low key, no parties or dates. Just me and Jon and some tasty delicious treats.

Snacks were very important to Jon and me, but we never really over-did it. We were kind of particular about what to eat and even more importantly, how will we obtain said-snack.

What adventure would await us?

What kinds of obstacles would we have to endure to get our bounty?

After much debate and deliberation, we developed a taste for some popcorn.

Not just any popcorn. No.

This had to be freshly popped and must, absolutely must have Molly McButter.

This was a problem, because we had tons of popcorn and a popcorn maker, but no Molly McButter.

Hmmmm...what to do.

We thought maybe our neighbors might have some.

"Knock-knock" on Tammy's door.

Tammy was the Snack Queen.

She always had stashes of Little Debbie, all kinds of Doritos, Frito's and Cheetos,

Pop tarts, both frosted, unfrosted and with and without sprinkles.

Oreos, hoho's, ding dongs, ring dings, Starbursts, Skittles, Snickers and anything with a Hershey's label.

"Hi Tammy, do you have any fake powdered Molly McButter?" I ask.

"Let me check," she says.

Jon looks hopeful, peering over my shoulder to see if Tammy was going to come through for us.

No luck.

She had cheese-flavored popcorn that was already popped, but no, that would not do.

"No thanks," Jon said, "We really want the fake powdered butter on hot popcorn."

"Powdered butter," Tammy said under her breath, "Powdered butter," she said again, looking on her shelves with one of her sausage-shaped fingers tapping her chin.

"I have powdered *donuts*…" Tammy said "And actual real butter" she offered.

"Thanks anyway, Tammy," Jon and I said in unison.

We went back to our room.

"We could go to the store and buy it," I said.

"Ok!" Jon said, "Let's get dressed."

Jon and I were now very excited about the prospect of selecting outfits to wear.

This enjoyable task took about 45 minutes.

I think one of the reasons Jon and I could snack on junk food and still fit into our little mini-skirts and skinny jeans is the simple fact that we expended more calories obtaining the food than the food itself.

It was kind of like the idea of eating celery.

They say the energy it takes to chew and digest it cancels out the calories when you eat it.

We laid out the various articles of clothing and decided on which one of us would wear which ensemble.

We changed out of our tank tops and boys boxer shorts into warm clothes.

It was winter in Flagstaff, but the dorms were hot, so everyone wore summer clothes indoors, even though it was 30 degrees outside.

We decided on tee shirts from Express, brightly colored oversized sweaters, leggings for Jon, jeans for me, and both of us wore socks that matched our respective sweaters. Big earrings, bangle bracelets and lots of decorative pins on our jean jackets.

"It's all about the accessories," Jon preached.

I nodded in agreement.

We always wanted to look adorable, even if it was just to go to Safeway and possibly Walgreens if Safeway didn't have Molly Mcbutter.

We had no luck in either store.

"Someone must have Molly McButter," Jon said.

"Do you want to go to Todd, Todd and Jeff's room?" I said, and then added, "It would be a shame not to be seen in these super cute outfits."

"Totally," Jon agreed.

So, off we went to Tinsley Hall.

Todd, Todd and Jeff were three guys we knew from freshman orientation.

This was how we met.

Jon noticed them and said to me "Those guys are staring at you, do you know them?"

I looked over and said, "No, I've never seen them before."

"They're walking over here," Jon said.

"Are you MaryJo?" one of the Todd's asked.

"Yeah," I said.

"We recognized you from your picture," the other Todd said.

Then Jeff piped up, "We're friends with Sean McDonald. He carries a photo of you in his wallet."

This information came as a surprise, but I didn't let on that there is not one substantial reason why Sean McDonald would keep a picture of me in his wallet.

Not one.

"Oh, yeah Sean McDonald. We dated for a little while," I said.

Sean McDonald was a drop-dead gorgeous, beautiful boy I had met over the summer at the Devil House.

This was the place to go if you wanted to dance all night in Tempe, AZ.

This is how we met.

I stood on a chair, looked over the crowd, spotted Sean and pointed at him.

I'd never asked guys to dance, but if you stand on a chair in a bar and point at someone, they come over to you!

Try it.

Sean McDonald marveled about how hot I was as we danced. He could not take his eyes off of me.

"You are so hot," he said as loudly as he could over the Thompson Twins song:

"You say I'm a dreamer, we're two of a kind
Both of us searching for some perfect world we know we'll never find
So perhaps I should leave here, yeah yeah go far away
But you know that there's nowhere that I'd rather be

than with you here
Today
Hold me now..."

He was captain of the swim team at his high school.

Why doesn't he already have a girlfriend, I wondered.

We went out a few times, but I had to break things off.

Here's what happened.

Sean had a really bad breakup with a girl named Christina.

They were a full-fledged couple for quite a while, as I understood.

Completely broken up and ready to start anew, Sean asked me out.

He had a handsome face with a swimmer's body. Strong, lean and muscular.

On one of our dates, we started kissing and he said it.

He called me the wrong name.

"Christina," He whispered.

"Uh, actually, it's MaryJo. We met earlier, remember?"

"Sorry," he says to me.

"That's ok, now get back here, where were we...." I said, ready to forgive and move on.

Anyone can make a mistake. Once.

We start kissing again and again he says

"Christina..."

"Sean," I say annoyed, "My name's not Christina, for crying out loud, are you kidding me?"

This is not going well at all.

I pulled away from him. I felt so used, so cheap. He was totally thinking of another girl while he was kissing me.

"I'm sorry, you see, Christina is my old girlfriend and I really miss her," he says, all sheepish and puppy-dog-eyed with a look that said please forgive me.

"Ok, I....I... guess I understand" I said, reluctantly, wishing he wasn't such a total fox.

Then, just when you think it's not going to get worse, he actually, really, genuinely said this to me:

"Would it be ok with you if I called you Christina when we kiss?"

"Sean," I said looking straight ahead in a very formal tone, "I believe this concludes our date."

What really bummed me out was the fact that Madonna's new song, *Crazy for You* came out and I really liked it and wanted a boyfriend so that could be our song.

"I never wanted anyone like this
It's all brand new, you'll feel it in my kiss
You'll feel it in my kiss because
I'm crazy for you"

"Oh, and by the way, Sean, thanks for ruining my Madonna song."

I never saw Sean again after that night.

I hadn't thought of him either, until I met Todd, Todd and Jeff.

Jon and I became friends with these boys. We hung out together. There was never anything but a superficial friendship between the five of us.

I think they instinctively knew that if I dated Sean, none of them would ever have a chance of dating me or my beautiful best friend, Jon.

The great thing is, Jon and I could always differentiate between the Todds without knowing their last names or using descriptions.

If one of us said that Todd, Todd and Jeff were coming over, we'd know it was the three of them.

But if we said Todd and Jeff were coming, we knew which Todd it was.

Really, there was the main Todd, and then the secondary, auxiliary back up Todd.

We'd go out to eat, go to movies and occasionally we'd rescue each other in one way or another.

Example: the phone once rang at 3am. It woke Jon and me out of a deep sleep. "Who is calling us in the middle of the night?" Jon and I asked each other.

I answered the phone.

"Heyyyyy MaryJo, it's Todd"

He was completely intoxicated.

Jon sat up in her bed.

"Ok, ok," I say, "Todd, honey, I will come and get you in a just a minute, stay there, stay."

"What's going on?" Jon asked, looking confused.

"Well, Todd's in our lobby. He's so drunk he can't find his dorm," I said as I slipped on my pink robe and fuzzy slippers, simultaneously wrapping my hair in a loose bun.

"That's terrible. Should we let him sleep on our floor?"

"Sure, I'll go get him. Be right back."

I walked Todd up the stairs to our room and he passed out on our floor. He left the next morning and we never mentioned it again. I don't think he even remembered the ordeal.

Anyway, on our quest for Molly McButter, Jon and I went to Tinsley Hall.

We appeared at Todd, Todd and Jeff's room, which was actually only Todd and Jeff's room, as they were better friends with each other than they were with the second Todd.

The door was open. They were having a party.

Jon and I walked in.

Several guys were sitting at a table playing poker, a few people were in a corner playing "Quarters" with shots of vodka and Jack Daniels.

Tears for Fears was on full blast.

"Shout, shout let it all out.
These are the things I could do without
Come on, I'm talking to you, so come on"

Jon asked Todd if they had any Molly McButter?

"What does she look like?" Todd asked.

"No, it's not a person, it's fake powdered butter sprinkles for popcorn," I yelled over the music.

"It's fat free," Jon added.

I nodded in agreement.

"Jeff, do you know some chick named Molly McDougal?" Todd asked.

Jeff was the pothead of the group. "Yeah, yeah, she just left a few minutes ago, I think she's coming back," Jeff says, offering me a plastic cup of warm beer that I declined.

 Jon and I took matters into our own hands and looked over the guys' snacks and did not see Molly McButter.

We barely even found any snacks.

Typical guys. Just some chewing tobacco, a pack of Marlboro Lights, some beef jerky, some turkey jerky, a can of tuna and a pack of Juicy Fruit gum.

As far as spices, "Just salt and pepper," Jon said, yawning.

"We really wanted hot popcorn with fake butter," I said to the guys.

 Then I went on to explain that we were extremely tired and could we please take a nap.

Jon pointed to a pile of blankets for Todd to get for us from the loft.

Jeff tossed us two pillows and Jon and I snuggled up in the corner for a little cat-nap. Right in the middle of their party.

Before college-life, Jon and I both had extremely strict curfews.

Now that we were on our own and could party all night, we were preconditioned to go to bed early, so no matter how hard we tried, we just couldn't stay up late.

We woke up a little while later and went back to our room.

By then it was too late for a movie and popcorn.

We just ended up putting on our tank tops and boxers and going to sleep.

"Want to go to Denny's for breakfast tomorrow?" Jon asked.

"Sure," I said, "Oh, What should we wear?"

Chapter 3
Clothing

"What's mine is yours!" Jon announced with absolute authority.

Ah, one of the great pleasures of rooming with your best friend: Sharing clothes.

Jon and I wore exactly the same size, so we both multiplied our wardrobe, virtually overnight.

We shared everything. Jeans, jackets, jump suits, shirts, skirts, shoes, blouses, belts, handbags, dresses, accessories, sweaters, swim suits, you name it.

Jon had excellent taste.

And her mom was a whiz with a sewing machine and had a fabulous flare for high fashion that would rival any couture connoisseur.

Jon's mom Sue would call regularly.

"Hello?" I answered.

"Hey MaryJo, it's Sue, is Jenny there?"

"Oh hi Sue!" I'd say, "Yes, she's here," Then I would go on to say how much we liked the clothes she sent us."

Sue became confused by this until Jon explained that we shared everything.

Jon also had an impressive shoe collection.

High tops, fringed boots, strappy sandals, pumps in every primary color, sling backs,

Mary Janes, mules, slides and flats. And gellies, lots and lots of gellies.

I believe she had a pair of shoes for every outfit.

I would put on one of Jon's lycra micro-mini skirt and leggings, my oversized man's collared shirt, two or three of her gigantic belts worn low on the hips.

She would study the outfit for a moment and then say, "I have just the right shoes for that."

She would then tie the whole outfit together with the perfect foot-ware every time.

Jon would even recommend the correct shoes for casual outfits such as the off–the-shoulder ripped sweatshirt with leggings, which I thought made me look *exactly* like Jennifer Beals in Flashdance.

I asked Jon,

"Don't I look exactly like Jennifer Beals in Flashdance?"

"Exactly," she promised.

Our room was like a mock department store. The collection of clothing was the envy of every girl in Allen Hall.

Our friend and next-door neighbor Tammy took a picture of us one day. We struck a model pose as soon as we saw the camera.

Tammy placed the picture on our door with a sign that said "The Vogue Babes Live Here."

Tammy always complimented us on our outfits.

"You're such Vogue Babes," She'd say as we walked by.

Super sweet.

Jon and I had so many clothes that we went a solid semester without doing even one load of wash.

Dirty laundry was piled to the ceiling, which explained why our door would only open part way.

One rainy day, we were bored and decided to do some loads of wash.

We separated the clothing and had a full load of each color.

I accidentally turned all of our whites purple. I think a sock sneaked its way in there.

We looked at the lavender clothes strewn on the floor, the beds and the desks.

"Hmmm," Jon said. "Well, I learned in my Design Class that ever primary color has a complementary color. And according to this color wheel, (click, click, click) green compliments purple.

"Jon! You are a genius!"

And that settled it. Off we went to the mall to buy some green clothes to match our new purple clothes.

Problem solved.

Even though we shared our clothes amicably, at least for a while, there were rules.

We still knew whose clothes belonged to whom, and on the rare occasion when one of the pieces of clothing became particularly beloved, or just plain looked better on one of us, that item became "sacred."

The item, however, had to be declared sacred in a verbal agreement. Discussions could take place, arguments were heard, and evidence would be presented.

Once the decision was made, though, we stuck with that rule.

Well, she did.

I once had a favorite shirt from The Limited. It was an oversized, white Forenza tee shirt.
Very cute.

I loved that tee. I looked great in that tee.

My mistake was that I did not declare it sacred.

Jon asked if she could wear the Forenza tee. I told her "No, sorry, it's dirty."

The next morning I wore the Forenza tee with a pair of robin's egg blue stretch pants and bright yellow flats. Totally cute.

Jon was infuriated and made a scene, demanding that I take it off immediately.

"First of all, those shoes don't go with those pants, and secondly, I thought the Forenza tee was dirty! Now, you are wearing it, you liar!"

She then pulled the shirt off my body leaving me in the Allen Hall third floor TV room in robin's egg blue stretch pants, bright yellow flats, and my bra.

"It's dirty?" She yelped.

"It's dirty?" I heard her the first time.

"Oh my God, you are crazy!" I said.

I paid for this mistake in many ways. Jon had clever ways of incorporating the word "dirty" into every conversation to make sure I knew I had made a grave mistake by lying to her.

If I asked her a question about anything in the following weeks, the answer was *"No, sorry, it's dirty."*

Never lie to Jon about clothes. It's just a bad idea.

Spring was in the air with just a hint of chill.

It was a great day to be alive, living in Allen Hall with my best friend. Sharing clothes.

Jon barged into the room and slammed the door.

"Who bothered you?" I demanded to know. I was not in the mood to hear how someone mistreated my precious friend.

"I went to get some milk for my cereal from the vending machine. As I walked down the hall, I heard laughter. It was two girls and I figured out they were laughing at me!" Jon said.

"They actually made fun of my outfit!" Jon said in total disbelief and utter confusion.

Jon had on an amazing ensemble of a canary gold tank top, yellow leggings, and an oversized periwinkle sweater dress.

And all of her accessories from her belt to her shoes, to her earrings matched.

Jon had a deeply held unshakeable conviction about matching her accessories to her outfits.

"They're just jealous," I said trying to console her.

Then I got angry and said, "Hey, wait a minute, half of that outfit is mine!"

That was the day we began truly hating mean girls. Not the girls themselves but their atrocious behavior.

We weren't the prejudiced types, in fact, Jon and I were all about embracing diversity.

Our philosophy was simple:

Gay? That's ok!

From a foreign country? No problemo!

Not into Christianity? Mazel tov!

But if you're a mean girl who makes fun of someone's outfit while she's walking down the hall to get milk from a vending machine for her cereal?

You better watch your back.

Example: Kelly was a mean girl from California. She had that awful nasal-valley-girl voice.

She was in our Introduction to Fabrics and Textiles class. Kelly and I were both Fashion Merchandising majors until I switched later to Communications.

She was your classic mean girl, but for some reason she wanted to be friends with Jon and me.

She once made our friend Tammy cry, because she said she was too fat to get into the Tri Deltas.

Rude.

This was one of the few classes Jon and I had taken together, so we enjoyed catching up during this time.

"When are you going to get over that cold, Kelly? You are always sick every time we see you." I asked her every time we saw her.

Jon would poke me and say, right in front of her "You always ask her if she's sick and she never is. That's really how she talks."

Kelly tried to hone in on our private talks, so I would have to distract her to get her to butt out.

"Kelly," I'd say slowly, "what is six times eight?"

I assigned this math problem to Kelly knowing it would buy Jon and me some time to talk more.

After a few minutes Kelly would say "eleventy-one."

"Right? Isn't six times eight eleventy-one?"

"I'm home," Jon said cheerfully.

"Man, that English Lit midterm was so hard. What are you doing?" She asked, while opening a carton of yogurt.

I held up the jar of unprocessed bran and with a wave of her hand, Jon declined.

"Oh, Betty the dorm janitor had a sign up asking for donations. Her daughter needs school clothes. She got a scholarship at Glendale Community."

It's the philanthropist in me. I like to help others" I said, piling clothes into a large box.

"Oh, that's so nice of you," Jon said.

Then she stood up and said, "Wait a minute, hold on, those are all my clothes."

"I know" I said, folding and dropping into the box.

"Stop!" she shouted. "Put them back, you freak, those are MY CLOTHES!"

Jon was angry.

"Jon, you never wear these."

And she goes "It doesn't matter, those are my personal belongings, you have no right!"

As I kept filling the box, she goes "Hey! My *Mom made* that!"

"She's gonna love these..." I said placing of more of Jon's clothes in the box.

This was the beginning of the end of our blissful-best-friends-clothes-sharing experience.

One morning I awoke to the sound of Jon coming into the room.

She was crying.

"What's wrong," I asked as I pulled the sheets up to cover my naked body, gesturing for Jon to hand me my lighter. I went through a stage where I slept naked.

And smoked.

"Well, I was walking to class," Jon started, and then blew her nose.

I took a very long drag on my cig, listening intently, thinking this better not involve a mean girl.

Jon motioned as if asking my permission to open a window.

I motioned back with my hand like that's fine.

Much of our communication was non-verbal.

"Anyway, you know how it is walking to South campus, on that bridge, well it's all icy today because of the storm last night," she went on.

Now she was sniffling and tearing more, "And I fell down."

"Oh my gosh, are you ok?" I asked as I flicked my ashes into a ceramic bowl.

"Ya, but then, all these stupid guys walked right by me and didn't even help me up.

I was so upset I got up and just decided to blow off my stupid class, which totally sucks because look how cute I'm dressed today," She said as she Q-tipped her running mascara.

"That is an adorable ensemble, what a waste."

She had on an airy-pink sweater over a cream button down blouse. A pastel floral jacquard mini skirt, off white tights and my Mark Alpert Italian leather boots in Vanilla.

Beautiful.

"What a bunch of jerks," I said trying to make Jon feel better.

"Yeah," Jon replied. Those guys were probably some losers I dated, then blew off.

"Yeah," I agreed.

Chapter 4
Shelter

"You need to live on the quiet floor,

You'll get more studying done," my Drill Sergeant told me as I was selecting living quarters for my first semester in college.

Not knowing any better, I obeyed this command and requested a room on the quiet floor of Allen Hall.

Jon and I did not belong on the quiet floor.

Mainly because we were very loud.

We proceeded to get in trouble every single day for being noisy.

I mean it.

Every single day.

Our laughter was too loud. Our hair dryers were too loud. Our stereo was too loud.

Our RA, Maggie, would pound on our door and say, "I love Stacy Q and Samantha Fox just as much as you do, but you girls are going to wake up the whole dorm! Please, *please* turn it down."

"Maggie is so sweet," I would say to Jon.

"I know, I don't know how she puts up with us."

"What Maggie just doesn't understand," Jon said, "Is the fact that the only way you'll wake up is if I blast the stereo."

So true. No alarm clock would work and Jon even tried kicking my bed and yelling at me to get up. I'm just a very heavy sleeper, always have been.

I simply had to have awesome 80's music playing at dangerous decibels or I would definitely oversleep.

Then I would miss my classes.

And fail out of college.

And I'm sure Maggie wouldn't want that.

So it was a must-have and we continued this practice out of necessity.

Then there was the constant laughter.
Our problem wasn't that we laughed too loudly. The real problem is that we literally found everything funny and couldn't control the laughter eruptions, which were usually accompanied by high-pitched screams.

This happened in the most inappropriate places.
Namely the laundry room, the TV room, the hallway or in our very own room.

Many times something would strike our funny bone in the hallway and we would run as fast as we could to get into our room, or the stairwell, whichever was closer, so we were not actually on the quiet floor when the noise came out of us.

One time we got "a talking to" by an RA named Bev for our unabashed disregard for the quietness of the quiet floor.

Jon spoke up very eloquently and said that technically we were not on the quiet floor when the alleged noise took place.

"We were in the stairwell, not on the quiet floor, right Jo?" Jon said to me in front of Bev.

"Absolutely, right, Jon, and good point," I answered.

I looked very concerned and say to Bev "Are you sure it was us?"

"Alright, you two, get back to your room and be quiet!" Bev said and walked away.

"We'll try Bev, we promise!"

We were told to keep our windows closed, as people were being disrupted from our giggling from all the way across the quad.

Every RA in Allen Hall knew us as the troublemakers in the dorm, and many meetings took place to discuss what they should "do with us."

One day Jon and I were walking out of the main lobby and we saw Maggie.

"Hey Maggie!" we chirped.

A feeling of guilt overtook us and we decided we should apologize for all of the grief we caused her.

"Maggie," I said "We just want you to know that we're really sorry for all the noise."

"Yeah," Jon added, "We really are sorry."

Our confession was quickly interrupted by lovely full-figured gal named Anna, with really long black hair.

"Are you Jenny and MaryJo?" she asked.

"Yes! We are!" we sang.

We were always pleased to be recognized.

Anna happened to be in some position of authority, and informed us that we were to move out of our room immediately.

She handed us a key which turned out to be for our new room and said "I want you two off the quiet floor today."

Wait a minute.

Hold on.

"First of all, we love your shoes," I said.

"And your hair," Jon said with a smile.

"She does have really good hair," I said to Jon.

Then I looked at Anna and said "Are you trying to tell us that we are being evicted from our room with absolutely no notice?"

"Yes, that's right, you have 12 hours to GET OUT. I meant it, I want you out of there."

"Really?"

Thank you!"

"We hate the quiet floor!" We said in unison.

We hugged Anna, took our key and ran off to pack.

After a few days in our new room on the not-so-quiet floor, we saw Leslie, our new RA.

We skipped and jumped over to her and introduced ourselves.

"I'm MaryJo and this is Jenny. You may have heard of us. We're a little loud."

"Where are you going?" Jon asked me, twice.

"Where are you going?" she asked a third time.

I ignored her.

It was well into our sophomore year and things seemed to be going just fine. I thought they were, anyway.

I was going to see Derek Jensen.

Derek Jensen was an elitist and conspiracy theorist who wore Armani suits and had the whitest teeth you have ever seen.

A junior at NAU, he took a great interest in healthy living, current events and lying.

He illegally sublet his dorm room, and somehow passed classes he never even showed up for.

He had a penchant for mostly white-collar crimes, but also stole an occasional vintage bottle of wine from the restaurant he managed.

And, irony of ironies, he was a criminal justice major.

I met Derek at our Accounting 211 midterm exam.

Earlier that day I told Jon I was scared to walk in the dark all the way to south campus and back for this exam.

She offered to drive and pick me up.

"No thanks," I said, "But can I take Esmerelda?

"Of course," she smiled.

Jon grabbed some paper and a pen. "What time do you think you'll be back?" She asks.

"Ten o'clock at the very latest," I said.

She handed me her keys and said to take good care of her.

Esmerelda was Jon's car. It was a 1973 white Toyota Celica. So cute, sporty and retro.

"Ok, if you're not home on time, I will call the campus police," she replied.

Jon and I always put each other's safety first.

I go to the exam, complete the test, hand it in. I begin walking to the parking lot.

Then, suddenly, there he was. Derek Jensen.

I thought he was extremely handsome so I started talking to him. We chatted it up for a while.

Dang, he is good looking, I thought.

He told me that he managed the Monte Vista Restaurant, and asked if I'd like a job there as a waitress.

It was a fancy, expensive place that served dishes like Chateaubriand for two, a big plate of meat that was lit on fire at your table.

Basically a meat fire.

"A job as a waitress? Sure," I said, "Sounds fun."

"First I would have to formally interview you. Are you free right now?" He asks.

He looked like an FBI agent who perhaps conducted sensitive national security investigations. Maybe foreign counter-intelligence or drug-trafficking matters.

He was impeccably dressed; his hair was carefully, yet purposely disheveled and gelled to perfection.

He reminded me a lot of a young James Spader, you know, the over-confident, sleazy, but hot best friend from "Pretty in Pink."

James Spader also played a very hot sleaze-ball in "Sex, Lies and Video Tape."

Yes.

Yes, I will get in this stranger's car in the middle of the night to go for a job interview.

Why not? What's the worst that could happen?

Keep in mind, Jon is expecting me back at our dorm room at 10pm, not a moment later.

Derek took me to The Monte Vista Restaurant. We sat across the table and he asked me a few questions.

"Have you ever waited tables before?"

"No."

"Have you ever worked in food service in any capacity?"

He asks, swirling his ice around in his glass and glancing around the room, looking more like James Spader now than ever.

"Um, nope."

"Do you like working with people?" he asks.

"Not really" I say.

"Could you start on Monday?" He asks.

"Ok, sure," I replied.

I was so excited about this fascinating new boy and my new job that I completely forgot to call Jon to tell her I'd be late.

I got home well after ten.

Jon had the campus police looking for me.

She was really mad. She had to sit there with Dennis Schmale, wondering where I was and was I ok.

"Where have you been?!" Jon yells at me.

She looked so panicked. I decided this would *not* be the right time to tell her about James Spader Guy.

Not the right time at all.

Dennis Schmale was a guy I had a date with that night.

He was so mad that he never called me again and Jon said that's ok because he looked like Robby Benson.

"Really? Do you really think he looks like Robby Benson?"

"Yeah, totally...he looks just like Robby Benson." Jon said.

Anyway, even though I didn't need to work, I became a waitress, solely for the purpose of being able to see Derek.

We became friends quickly.

We would talk for hours.

We'd talk about really important and interesting things like religion, philosophy and the human condition.

There was an incredible attraction between us.

After a couple of shifts at the restaurant, I ask him if he'd like to come over and watch a movie with me.

We went to my dorm room.

Jon was asleep in her bed.

I put "Officer and a Gentleman" in my rented VCR and we watched it on my tiny black and white TV.

I always made boys watch that movie. It's kind of my trademark.

So, we watched the movie.

The whole movie.

From beginning to end.

He didn't try to kiss me, or anything.

Finally, baffled, I whisper, "Are you interested in me at all?"

"Yes." He says.

"Ok...so, then, like, why don't you try to kiss me?" I asked, embarrassed.

We were speaking ever so quietly as to not wake Jon.

Then he says something that cuts right through my heart' "There's a girl in California with my name all over her."

"You're married!" I whisper-scream.

"No, I'm not married, but I have a serious girlfriend," he says, rubbing his face with both hands.

"Then why are you on my bed watching Officer and a Gentleman with me, if you have a girlfriend?" I say, now sitting up and thinking how dare he ruin my movie.

Still rubbing his face and eyes.

"I would like you to leave." I say, as Richard Gere carries Debra Winger out of the factory.

It was now 3am.

Derek leaves.

I plop onto my bed, feeling very alone.

I needed my best friend.

Suddenly Jon pulls her covers off her and jumps out of bed.

"I heard the whole thing! What a jerk, oh my Gosh!" She yelps.

"Oh, good" I say, not at all upset that she was listening.

"That saves me from having to tell you what happened," I say, a little relieved.

"Totally," Jon says. Then she added "Get dressed, we're going to Denny's."

We put on scarves, gloves and coats over our pajamas.

I am stunned.

Stunned.

We get to Denny's.

All I can do is light my cigarette, slam my lighter on the table, and look at Jon like "Can you believe that guy?"

"Total loser," Jon says.

I chained smoked waiting for the waitress to bring our eggs, bacon, biscuits, toast, coffee and hot fudge sundaes.

Jon was right. Derek was a total loser.

But that didn't stop me from seeing him.

Often.

Really often.

Like, every minute of every day. It was a sick compulsion.

We would eat breakfast, lunch, and dinner. Together.

We did our laundry together.

We skipped our classes together.

We'd lie on my bed listening to Sam Cooke tapes for hours, with the windows open and the scent of pine trees and pheromones permeating the room.

To this day if I hear that soulful sound of Sam Cooke's voice, I become transported to that time.

A time of wonder, excitement, sexual frustration and intoxicating fear.

Fear that I'd lose Derek.

Fear that I will never feel this way again about any man.

Derek was very different from anyone I had ever known.

He was timeless.

He seemed like he was from a different era and was somehow transported into my present day.

On the NAU campus, if you saw Derek, you saw me. We were absolutely inseparable.

In the time I knew Derek, I don't believe I looked at clock even once.

We'd drive all the way up to the mountains in his truck and park in a meadow.

It was fantastic.

Just us, talking, listening to music, enjoying the crisp clean mountain air and looking at the stars.

It really felt like we were the only people on the planet. And that was fine with us.

I spent so much time and energy on Derek, that I completely neglected every other human being and responsibility in my life.

You know, like a sociopath.

Nothing else mattered and no one else existed.

I'd get home as the sun was rising and Jon would say "Do you have any idea what time it is?"

"Not now Jon, I have to get some sleep, Derek's picking me up for breakfast in like, ten minutes."

People thought we were dating.

"Dating? No!" we laughed.

Then, it happened.

A very bad thing happened.

Lana moved to Flagstaff.

Lana was the girl in California that "Had his name all over her."

Why did she have to have such a sexy name?

There was a knock on the door. Jon answered it, looked at me in horror she said "Derek's here."

I was not in tune at all with Jon's visual cue that something was terribly wrong, so I naturally swung the door open wide to see him.

In a very Lifetime-Movie-Event-for-Women sort of way, Derek brought Lana to my dorm to introduce us.

I know this sounds dumb, but she didn't really seem like a real person.

In my mind, she was just a stick figure. Just a stick figure with no face.

She barely even had a name, in my mind.

Nevertheless, there she stood.

In between me and happiness.

"Lana, this is Jo." Derek said.

In total shock, but remembering my manners, I extend my hand to shake hers.

And here's what my thought bubble looked like:

"Oh my God, that's the woman he's in love with."

"That's the reason I can't be with him, forever and always."

"That's the cause of my misery."

"She must die."

"DIE."

I willed her dead with one really hard blink of my eyes.

She was still there.

Still alive.

Alive and dating my boyfriend.

Lana was very tall, I dare say statuesque.

She was curvy and stylish and did I mention tall?

She looked and sounded like a CNN newscaster.

She even had the signature journalist's blond bob hairstyle, and drove a Mercedes.

Her voice was strong and confident and it seriously sounded like she was going to let us all know about the unrest in the Middle East, and coming up, weather: big storms headed this way for all you Midwesterners. But first, let's get a look at sports.

She articulated every syllable to death and enjoyed using big words like "animosity, confrontation and escalation."

At this very first meeting, where I was introduced to what we will now call my nemesis, I find out a very interesting fact.

Lana was completely shocked to meet me.

Then, she says it.

"Jo?"

She looks at Derek and says this:

She goes "Jo is a *girl*?"

I looked down at my outfit, which was definitely not something a boy would wear, and shot a look at Jon, like 'Why would she say that?'

I wore a bright pink sweater from Express, bright pink leggings and a flouncy hound's-tooth mini skirt with a wide elastic waist. Black flats. Adorable. And girly.

Of course I'm a girl.

Of course.

I had the hair scrunchies and lip gloss collection to prove it.

I was the ultimate girl.

A bona-fide, card-carrying member of the sisterhood.

My manicure was never, under any circumstances chipped or faded.

All of my panties matched my bras.

All of them.

Am I a girl? Who would dare question this. Who?

I am the original Primp Queen!

And now this person was questioning the authenticity of my girl-ness?

What?

And newsflash, FYI, heads-up and a P.S. – I owned 300 bottles of nail polish.

That's right, three hundred.

Jon shrugged and shook her head like she didn't know what this was about either.

Then it hit me. Derek would be on the phone with Lana and I would hear him say things like "I went out to lunch with my friend, Joe."

Or "My buddy, Joe and I studied in the library together."

Poor Lana did what any of us gals would do and assume he was talking about a GUY.

Why. Why. Why would she think differently?

He was such a liar.

The worst king of liar.

A liar who lied by omitting very critical information like the fact that his friend Jo is a hot brunette.

At that time, it didn't matter that he was a completely fraudulent and a dishonest sleazy person.

I was in too deep.

I don't know what it was, but for some unknown reason, I was completely attracted to him.

I would have felt bad for Lana, but the fact is, it was game on.

I still wanted him.

She had him.

As far as I was concerned, she was toast.

Things did become physical between Derek and me. There was a whole lot of making out.

Jon was very disgusted with the whole situation.

"So, let me get this straight," Jon says, sitting at her desk, as she puts her pencil in her Psychology 101 textbook and closes it.

Then she goes on, "He has a girlfriend, but he spends all of his time with you."

"No, you don't understand," I said, "We don't sleep together, we don't have sex."

Jon picked up the latest issue of Glamour and pointed to an article "No, see, it's called 'emotional cheating' she says.

"He's bad news. You deserve better," Jon would say over and over.

And I did deserve better.

"I swear he just likes to be seen with you because you're so pretty," Jon said.

"Oh, thank you," I smiled and smoothed my hair while looking in the mirror.

I had talked to Derek about the situation.

I didn't act desperate or make demands. I simply said to him,

"You know, just thinking out loud here, sharing ideas, brainstorming, I know you're with Lana, but what if you broke up with her?

No chance of that, he promised.

Then one evening, Jon reached her breaking point.

That's when Jon kept asking me "Where are you going?"

I ignored her.

I was going to see Derek.

I pretended not to hear her. She was like this irritating fly buzzing around me.

"Leave me alone." I say.

"No. Where are you going?" she demanded.

Then in the hallway, she grabs my shoulders and pins me to the wall.

"MaryJo," she says "He doesn't love you. He's not going to leave her. You have to stop."

"Stay out of it!" I yelled at her.

Then I started crying.

I really tried to get Jon off me.

I pushed her arms away and she came back full force. She's small, but she's strong.

"Stop this. Stop. Stop. I mean it. You are 19 years old! You are too old for this! Don't do this," she pleaded.

I wanted to stop it.

I really did. Like a drug addict on that show "Intervention."

I needed help.

Now I was crying harder.

I began to lose strength, both physically and emotionally.

I began sobbing, uncontrollably. I was letting every bit of emotion out that I held in for months. I'd lost control.

My toothbrush and Pepsodent fall to the floor.

"You have to stop. You have to." She says.

I slid down the wall. Jon crouched in front of me and said, "I care too much about you to see you go down this path."

At this point I was in a heap on the floor.

Jon had a look on her face I hadn't ever seen before. It was pure defiance.

She was not letting go. She still had my shoulders pinned.

She instinctively knew if she moved, I still would have made a run for it.

Out of my peripheral vision, I saw a few girls walk by in their bathrobes, carrying their shower caddies to and from the bathroom.

They were staring, pretending not to notice. Whispering.

I don't know what they thought.

Maybe they wondered if they had a friend as special and good as Jon.

A friend who treasured her best friend enough to not care what this scene looked like.

A friend who wanted only good things for her very best friend.

Jon picks me up and walks me to her bed. I lay there, in fetal position. I was drained.

The ache in my chest was horrendous. My face burned from my tears.

I heard Jon on the phone across the room. I can see her, but my vision was all blurry.

"Is she having me committed?" I thought.

"Hi Stan, I need you to come over right away and bring 2 pints of Haagen Dazs.

One strawberry and one chocolate chip."

I groaned and she goes "Make that mint chocolate chip."

She sounded like she was calling in a prescription for heavy-duty meds.

Stan was a guy I went out with a few times. All of my friends called him "Me-Stan" because whenever he called me he'd say "Hi, MaryJo, it's me, Stan."

So Kara would be like "Me-Stan is on the phone for you."

One time Kara goes "Wouldn't it be funny if everyone announced themselves like that?"

And then as we were watching the nightly news Kara goes "Live, from the Holy Land, it's Me, Tom Brokaw."

Kara actually said something funny! Good for her, I remember thinking.

Stan was from India and would do anything for me.

And he was a genius...I'm not kidding. I was actually partially attracted to him for his math skills.

And so nice. He once bought me a really great outfit for no reason at all. I told him I couldn't accept such an expensive gift, because I didn't really have strong feelings for him.

So I gave the outfit back.

Well, I gave the top back. I kept the skirt because I looked smoking hot in it.

"You have to keep that skirt," Jon said when I showed it to her.

I had to break up with Stan because when I saw "Pretty in Pink" I didn't feel at all like Molly Ringwald did when Andrew McCarthy kissed her at the very end of the movie.

She was so enraptured in the kiss, she dropped her handbag and didn't even care.

Stan showed up with the Haagen Dazs, two spoons, and a bouquet of pink roses, my fave, asking if I was ok, and what was wrong.

I was on lock-down.

Jon thanked Stan and told him I needed my rest, and that he could call me later.

Jon stayed up with me all night. She never left my side while I went through my Derek Jensen Detox.

She even gave me half of her ice cream when I finished mine.

She was right, I would get over him.

The sun would rise again.

I would smile again. I would trust again.

I often wonder, what would have happened if I didn't have my angel.

My best friend, Jon.

"You'll end up hating each other," was the phrase we heard most often when we told people we were best friends planning to become roommates.

Jon and I ignored the warnings and went ahead with our arrangements to share a dorm room.

Things started out great, but it really is difficult to share a 15 foot by 15 foot cube with one sink, one tiny fridge, one mirror and every single article of clothing, best friends or not.

We used to stand at our tiny mirror in the morning elbowing each other out of the way, while putting on our makeup.

That, by the way, was how Jon came up with the name Primp Queen.

"We are such Primp Queens," she'd say, while applying her mascara.

And I would nod in agreement as I glossed my lips.

Our relationship became strained but I didn't like the alternative of living with someone else.

Jon asked me to lunch one day. We went to a very classy salad place in the mall. It was a sit-down restaurant with white table clothes and sparkling silverware. Nice.

"Jo, I wanted to talk to you about something," Jon said as the waiter placed our breadbasket on the table.

"What's up?" I asked, as I picked my lemon wedge out of my water glass, poured salt on it and took a huge bite.

Her eyes filled with tears as she fumbled with her fork and spoon.

"Jon, what is it? Is there something wrong?" I asked, growing nervous.

"Jo, I love you and I always want to stay best friends, that's why I can't live with you anymore."

I breathed a sigh of relief that she wasn't terminally ill or pregnant.

"Oh," I said. "Ok, that's fine." I was hurt.

"What if I quit smoking and start wearing pajamas?" I offered.

"No, it's not that, it's not even that you poisoned me with fiber or donated half my wardrobe to the dorm janitor," she went on, "I think we just need to live in separate rooms.

"This is about the stationary, isn't it?"

"No, no, it's really not, Jo" Jon said.

When Jon went home for a few months due to a serious bout with mono, I wrote her letters daily.

I used every single piece of personalized stationary she had gotten for a gift for high school graduation. It had her initials in gold and she rationed each piece carefully, as to not waste it.

I also used her entire pre-paid calling card to make long distance calls to her, Gram, my brother, David at UCSD and his roommate, Stewart, when David wasn't there.

I think the proverbial straw that broke the camel's back was when she'd get home from a date and I would greet her with the zeal of a TV game show host.

"Well! Good Morning! My goodness you have been out late! It's almost time for breakfast!"

She couldn't take it anymore.

I can't say I blame her.

After a long talk at lunch that day, we both agreed that this would be the best way to stay "best friends."

Jon loved sharing her room with Katherine, sweet, plain, quiet girl from Alaska.

Which, no offense, explained her wardrobe.

I roomed with Kara, our friend from the second floor.

"Well, I guess that's the last of it," Jon said, holding a box of her belongings.

"Oh, and I want my black bikini and my Debbie Gibson tape back," she said as she stood there waiting for me to respond.

"Really, I really do want them back," she added. Waiting.

I was too bummed to get out of bed.

I half-heartedly pointed to my dresser.

She put the box down just long enough to grab those last two items out of my drawer.

"It's really for the best," Jon said to me, "You'll see."

Jon looked at Kara and said "Good luck with her!" and closed the door with her foot.

Good luck with her?

What was that supposed to mean?

Jon was gone.

Well, she was just down the hall, but it seemed so far away.

And that same day, Kara moved in.

Kara thought she was very cosmopolitan. She was really cute. Picture a young blonde Natalie Wood. A natural beauty.

"Are you going to put any makeup on today, Kara?" I'd ask her.

"I am wearing makeup," she'd say. I would get really close up to her face and say "Oh, yeah, I guess you are."

But she always had bags under her eyes and was running late for one appointment or another.

She was involved in many clubs and associations on campus, a writer and editor of the school newspaper, straight A student, and never had any fun.

Kara was a serious work-a-holic who believed that spontaneity had its time and place.

She also had this annoying habit of breaking into a British dialect in conversation.

She wasn't trying to be cute or funny. I think she really thought she was from England some times.

"Would you like some toast and jam?" She's say in her fake accent.

"Aren't you from Sacramento?" Jon would say.

She listened to classical music and read thick, serious books.

When she wasn't irritating me, she was boring me to death.

I was the anti-Kara.

One evening she was sitting on her bed and looked especially sad.

"What's up, Kara?" I asked, hoping she'd say it was nothing.

"There's a formal for The Spurs," she said.

The Spurs National Honor Society are a sophomore service organization.

A side note and interesting fact: Every Friday the members of The Spurs were required to wear their uniforms, these really uncomfortable, stuffy Navy blue suits.

If anyone failed to wear their suit, the President of the club would issue them demerits.

Kara was the president of the club.

And all of The Spurs knew I was her roommate.

So, when I was walking around campus, if I caught any Spur wearing regular clothes on a Friday, they'd beg me not to tell Kara.

I didn't tell Kara and probably wouldn't have told her because I really didn't care about such things, but it was an easy way for me to make a few bucks.

I would put my hand out and say "You know the rules," and they had to give me five dollars to keep quiet.

Anyway, Kara had a formal event to attend. Normally she wouldn't be caught dead doing something like this, as it would be against her nature to have a good time, but she was required to go to this as the President.

"So, what's the problem?" I asked, pouring myself a sorely needed vodka tonic.

Kara begins crying. She tells me that the problem is she cannot get a date to save her life.

"I have to go to this event, and nobody wants to be my date!" she wailed.

This sounded serious.

Kara and I were not close friends, but I felt it was my duty to be there for her.

It was so sad; suddenly she seemed so little, and vulnerable, like a child.

"Want me to come up?" I asked.

She nodded her head yes and I crawled up onto the upper bunk of the loft.

We built our own loft for our room. Well, sort of.

We flirted with the guys at the lumberyard and they ended up coming over and putting it together for us, for free.

So nice.

Kara and I sat cross-legged on her bed facing each other. This position was generally reserved for Jon and me, but I made an exception.

I leaned back down, grabbed my cocktail, an extra cup and a box of tissues.

I poured half my vodka tonic into the cup and handed it to her.

"Ok," I said, resting my chin on laced fingers. "Let's strategize."

Now she had the hiccups from crying so hard but started to calm down.

"You need a date for the formal," I began.

"Do you want me to call one of my boyfriends to see if they can take you?" I asked.

Then I added "Me-Stan would be glad to take you, or one of my military guys, or there's that one guy I met in the dining hall, I forget his name, or the guy who's taking me to the Sizzler tomorrow night, Phil or Bill or something...What do you say, do you want one of my boyfriends?

"No. Thank you," she said. "I really want to go with someone who kind of likes me? You know? I want a little bit of romance."

The truth was, there were guys who did like Kara, but she put off such an ice-princess vibe, they were terrified to ask her out.

And she said "no" so many times, they were tired, almost exhausted from getting turned down time and time again.

"What about that Vince guy, you know from that place you go every day?"

"You mean work?" she asks, then adds "He has a girlfriend now."

"Ok," I said, pausing to sip my cocktail.

"What about that guy, what's his name, from your advertising copy writing class?"

Kara got a dimly lit sparkle in her eye.

"You mean...Brian?" she hiccupped.

She softly said, "You know, I forgot about him, he's really sweet and cute. He once asked me to go to a George Winston concert, but I had too much homework."

A couple days later Kara came back to the room and told me Brian was thrilled to take her to the formal. She was so happy.

"I'll do your makeup for you, too." I said and hugged her.

"Oh thank you MaryJo, that would be lovely," she said. (British accent).

Fall was upon us. The leaves were changing, the air was deliciously crisp.

I had just seen the greatest film of all time, Dirty Dancing, and desperately wanted a pair of cutoff jeans like "Baby" wore in the movie.

I had the perfect plan to get those cut offs.

I barged into Jon and Katherine's room, threw open Jon's closet door and began searching for a good pair of jeans.

"Oh, hi, MaryJo," Katherine said. "Jenny's not here, she went to Phoenix for the weekend."

"Oh, that's ok, Kat. Jon and I share everything. She won't mind if I just borrow these jeans," I said with a big smile.

Katherine then nervously explained that she was specifically told not to let anyone borrow anything of Jon's while she was gone.

"Ah, I found them....the perfect pair." I plucked the jeans off the hanger and prepared for my departure.

"See ya Kat! Have a good one. By the way, did you see Dirty Dancing?" I asked. "You need to see that movie!"

After I found a good, sharp pair of scissors and the perfect white tee shirt, I proudly wore my new outfit, and I got a lot of compliments all day.

The next day I went to the Learning Assistance Center, wearing my jeans again, where I was getting tutored for my math class.

Alex was my tutor.

He was kind of cute, and he really, really cared that I knew the many differences between complex and linear differential equations.

It was absolutely endearing, and I just loved him for it.

"Are you MaryJo?" the receptionist asked me.

"Yes." I said

"You have a phone call," She replied.

I went to the phone and it was Kara, my roommate.

"MaryJo, Jenny came by the room and left a note for you," Kara said.

Then she added, "I think you should come home and read it."

"Well, what does the note say, Kara?" I asked, annoyed.

"I can't read it to you because I don't use that kind of language," she said.

I told Karen I'd be there shortly and started packing my book bag.

"Alex, I have to go."

"But you have a test tomorrow..." He pleaded.

"I'll be fine. You taught me well...you put the coefficient next to the function constant and take the variable and carry the one," I said, then I tweaked his nose.

"Hey, Alex, do you want to go on a picnic with me next weekend?" I asked, as I was halfway out the door.

"Yeah!" he said, pushing his glasses up on the bridge of his nose, "Yes, I would really like that."

I had a terrible habit of asking guys questions like this, where it appears to be a date, but no.

No, there were twenty other people there. Random friends.

I left the Learning Assistance Center and walked back to my dorm room.

"Hey, Kara," I said, putting my book bag down.

"It's right there.

"The note," she said, pointing.

I pick it up.

One, two, three...six times she used the F word.

She didn't sign her name but I knew it was from Jon.

She wrote in really big letters when she was mad.

All caps.

I went to see her immediately.

Just as she started her accusatory tirade, she looked down and saw that not only did I steal her jeans, but I also had cut them.

I tried to explain the situation.

She was so mad, that while she was screaming at me, her face turned red and little beads of spit welled up in the corners of her mouth.

During this meeting, I found out incidentally, that she had *not* seen Dirty Dancing.

After she stopped yelling at me, I looked at her with complete sincerity and said "Jon, is this because the jeans look better on me?"

Jon crossed her arms, turned her back and stood there fuming.

"Well," offering what I thought was a very good consolation, "You know, you can borrow them any time you want."

"Borrow them..." she started, "Are you out of your mind?" (Rhetorical.)

She was so angry that she said she couldn't even talk to me anymore.

"Any more right now, or any more ever?" I asked for clarification.

As Jon stomped away from me in disgust, I yelled to her "Hey, is that a new top?"

I thought she was waving at first, but turns out she was giving me the finger.

"Can I borrow it sometime?"

She kept walking.

She didn't look back even once.

"My dress is here!" Kara screeched.

She walked in with a gigantic box and ripped it open with excitement.

It was a strapless, black silk organza gown her mom made for her to wear to The Spurs formal. Layer upon layer of luxurious fabric.

After the arduous, toilsome, exhausting undertaking of securing a date for Kara, the big night was finally upon us.

She put the gown on, slipped into her black pumps and began dancing like a Prima Ballerina. She looked like a princess.

"Oh, I feel so pretty!" she beamed and twirled. She was even smiling.

It was so out of character from the freakishly serious wallflower I grew to almost like a little bit.

Her friend Janet was there to take pictures of Kara in her gown.

Kara walked into the hallway so all of the girls in the dorm could admire her.

The girls Ohhhed and ahhhed and they told Kara how beautiful she looked.

"It's just a dress," I said, sipping my vodka tonic.

Janet lowered her camera from her eyes and glared at me like I was being rude.

I shrugged my shoulders and fake smiled.

"Hey! I got it, I'll put my prom dress on." I said.

"NO. MaryJo, don't you dare." Kara hissed.

Just after I put my high school prom dress on, the phone rang.

There I stood, in a formal gown, gloves, sparkling jewels and pumps.

"Hello?" it was some guy named Brad.

"Am I available to attend a military ball tonight? Why, yes, yes I am!" I said as I looked at Kara like, wow, all I did was dress up and presto: Date!

Brad had a military formal to attend that evening and unfortunately his date fell through.

"Do you have any references?" I asked, motioning for Kara to get me a pen and paper.

Turns out Brad was a friend of my Drill Sergeant, so I decided yes, I'll go!

"Can you believe we BOTH have formals this evening?" I asked Kara in disbelief.

"Now I know why Jenny hates you so much," she said.

Between my sophomore and junior year in college, I decided it would be super fun to go to summer school.

And I was right.

My parents said I could stay up at school if I could somehow get free room and board, so I applied to become a Resident Assistant.

I got the job. Free food and housing all for doing virtually nothing.

I just had to make sure the girls in the dorm didn't keep pets in their rooms, drink themselves to death, burn the place down with their hot plates, or make too much noise.

They basically could do whatever they wanted because, well, I really didn't take the job too seriously.

I spent that magical summer taking two classes, which occupied exactly 5 hours a week, and the rest of the time I played volleyball and went out partying every night.

I had morning classes that allowed me to get back to my dorm room just in time to grab a snack and catch "The Young and the Restless."

After that I'd sit in my room smoking, listening to Blondie tapes over and over, and write in my journal.

I made some new friends, too.

Jon left NAU to go take care of her mom and I was tired of sitting around feeling sorry for myself.

At first when Jon left, I took it pretty hard.

I stayed in my room alone and wouldn't talk to anyone.

I went to class, to the dining hall, then back to my room. Same thing every day.

I stayed in on weekends.

Finally, my neighbor, Tammy knocked on my door and wouldn't stop until I answered.

"What," I said, answering the door in my bathrobe, vodka tonic in my hand.

"Good Morning! Hey, put your bikini on right now, we're all lying out in the quad." She said all bubbly.

"No," I said, shutting the door on her while she tried to persuade me.

If Jon wasn't around, I wasn't interested in talking to anyone.

Anyway, summer school began and it was time for me to get out and have some fun.

NAU is an absolute blast in the summer. The weather is amazing. The fresh mountain air was almost intoxicating, and the rain showers were romantic.

Lots of thunder and pounding rain.

Then after a few minutes, it would stop and the sun would be out again.

We slept in. We stayed out late. We went to the movies.

We wore shorts and tank tops and flip-flops and cut-off jeans like Baby in Dirty Dancing.

Everyone was dating everyone.

People would hook up, then it was if someone yelled "Rotate!" and the partners would get switched.

It was like R-rated square dancing.

It was twenty-four hours of fun, fun, fun till Daddy took the T-bird way.

I made friends with a girl in my dorm named Judy.

Judy had an adorable, petite figure and a perfectly proportioned face.

Her blonde ringlets went on for miles, and one lock of hair would always fall right in front of one of her enormous blue almond-shaped eyes.

She would coyly dip her chin and talked so softy you had to lean in to hear her.

She whispered everything, kind of like Marilyn Monroe.

Guys went crazy over Judy.

Judy really taught me that it's ok to truly embrace my sensual, feminine, mysterious side.

She savored everything whether it was a cup of coffee, a juicy steak, or a stick of Wrigley's.

"Mmmmmm, this gum is *soooooooo* good," she'd purr.

She literally gave me sexy lessons.

Judy was earthy and touch-feely and artsy.

She would arch her back, push her hair back with her hand so you could see her thumb ring, swing one leg over the other when she sat down, clasping her hands over the exposed knee.

She'd giggle at guys' jokes even when I knew for a fact she didn't really get them.

Judy almost always had a look on her face like she just had the best orgasm of her life.

The other times she looked like she was about to say something extremely thoughtful, almost profoundly important.

Waiting...waiting.

Nope, it was just her look.

Then she went back to the orgasm face.

Judy was gorgeous and sexy but not without a quirky side.

For instance, she didn't like the way she sounded when she said certain words so she would spell them out.

Specifically she didn't like words that started or ended in the letter "R."

Luckily this only applied to proper nouns.

This made conversations confusing at times, but eventually I got used to it.

"I went out with R-o-y last night," She'd say.

One Friday afternoon, I got the idea to get all dolled up and go out. I wanted to go to some of the local bars and flirt and have fun.

I call Judy.

"We could go out, she said, but we can't get into bars because you're not 21," she said.

"Judy, we're going out!" I say with total optimism and enthusiasm.

I was craving a good time.

What I really truly wanted was a boyfriend.

I wanted to meet the man I would spend the rest of my life with. I wanted a connection of Titanic proportion. (the song, not the ocean liner.)

I wanted love, inside jokes, and laughter that made my heart swell.

I wanted to be the movie Wuthering Heights. Only, you know, a different ending.

I wanted to be so close to someone that they would think, "I know you, I really know you," without having to say it out loud.

I wanted someone who would only say "I love you" once and never need to again, because I would already know it and feel it from the way he treated me and looked at me.

I wanted someone who ignored all my bad qualities and prized my good ones.

I wanted someone to go to weddings with so I didn't have to sit at the singles table, or worse, the kids' table.

I wanted someone I could bring to Thanksgiving, and then make fun of my family with me on our way home.

Someone I could put make-up on sometimes if I felt like it.

I wanted someone who knew when I scratch my head with both hands it means I am ready for my nap.

I wanted someone who knows when I'm sick I only want toast, Chips Ahoy cookies, (the crunchy kind, not the soft kind) and Fruit Punch flavored Gatorade that must be ice cold, but cannot actually have any ice in it.

I wanted someone to put their arm around me when we walked so my shoulder would fit perfectly under their arm and it would feel safe and warm and good.

He's out there, somewhere.

I spent a long time getting ready that day for my night out.

It took a lot of time and energy to make myself look like I didn't put too much time and energy into it.

Effortlessly-flawless-sexy-gorgeous-beautiful-interesting was the look I was going for.

I wore a black mini-dress and black strappy high-heeled sandals.

I looked awesome.

Judy and I went to Fiddlestix, a local bar that was impossible to get into without ID.

She was skeptical about our plan.

"Come on Judy, we're going in," I say, putting on an extra coat of black eye liner.

Outside of Fiddlestix, a line of about 15 people stood in front of a bouncer that looked a lot like Dog, the Bounty Hunter. Only not as friendly and much bigger.

Judy and I walk to the front of the line.

Judy arches her back, looks at the bouncer and whispers "I work here." And he lets her in.

She doesn't have to pay the cover charge, show ID, or anything.

Genius.

But now, where does that leave me.

I had exactly two seconds to formulate a plan.

I put my hand on Dog's shoulder as if to push him out of my way and I say, "Excuse me."

Miraculously he lets me in, too!

It was a gamble.

I made it in.

I see a large table of guys so I walk over. It's my Drill Sergeant with several of his Delta Chi frat brothers.

I sit with them, they buy me drinks. We talked and laughed. A few of them asked me out.

I said yes, yes and yes.

Meanwhile, Judy leaves which is fine because she's hotter than me.

I didn't want her messing up my new sex-vibe.

I notice a group of guys walking toward me. One of them looks at me and say's "Hi Mary."

Uhg! Did he just call me MARY.

That's not my name, so I do not answer him.

I ignore him, turning around, flipping my long dark hair.

I went home that night with sore feet from dancing and a few dates lined up for the following week.

Oh, well, I didn't meet the man of my dreams tonight, I thought, maybe it won't happen for a long time.

I can wait.

I loved being an R.A.

Free housing and free food, all for doing virtually nothing.

In addition to eating in the dining hall with my free food card, I also went to the Snack Shack every day.

Barb was the clerk at the Snack Shack, the little convenience store on campus.

She was an older lady and a real grouch.

She never smiled and looked like she ate college students for lunch.

"Hi Barb!" I'd sing as I went in to get my treats.

At first she ignored me, or scowled something unintelligible, but no worries, I was there to get my sweet tooth satisfied.

Part of enjoying the snack is the experience of going to get it. I always made a point to smile and ask Barb just how she's doing today.

And she was always doing "Terrible."

"What should I get?" I say to Barb, as I walked up and down the aisles of brightly colored packages. "Maybe something salty, like chips?"

Barb stood halfway out the door so she could smoke her cigarette.

Ignoring me.

"Or, should I go for something cold, like Haagen Dazs?" I asked her as she pretended not to hear me.

She blew a smoke ring and says in a very Marge Simpson's Sister voice "Have you seen the new manager at the dining hall?"

Barb is talking to me...Yay!

"No," I say, putting my single pack of Oreos on the counter and opening my purse, "Why, what's wrong with him?"

Always and forever interested in a juicy dish, I was all ready to get the scoop from Barb.

"Nothing's wrong with him," she says, "He's really hot."

"Um, Barb, no offense, but my version of hot is probably not the same as yours." I say.

"No, he's gorgeous," she says.

He's young. From Chicago. A real fox. And so nice." She says, putting her cig out so she can ring up my order.

"Does Mr. Wonderful have a first name?" I ask.

"I don't know his name, but if I were 20 years younger I'd take him and...." She went on.

"Whoa! Ok, Barb, calm down, that's enough," I said.

"You should meet him," she says.

"Nah, not interested in some old guy that wears polyester pants and probably has coffee breath to beat the band," I say and turn up my nose.

"No." I add just in case she kept pushing.

A few days later I go into the dining hall.

It was the night after I got into Fiddlestix and had an absolute blast. I met so many cute guys.

Someone is standing in front of the coffee bar.

What's this?

A young man wearing a pink oxford button down shirt, a tie and dress pants.

He had a V shape athletic build, a sexy slim waistline and shoes that looked kind of pricey.

"Hi," I say.

"Hi," the young man says.

Internally I felt a feeling I'd never felt before.

It was a jolt of electricity, but something else.

The only way to put it into words is this, I felt like "Oh, there you are."

He seemed familiar to me, but I knew we hadn't met.

"Are you the new manager of the dining hall?" I ask.

"Yes," he says, as cannot stop staring into his beautiful blue eyes.

"I'm MaryJo," I say and shake his hand. "I heard you're a total babe and I should meet you."

"Craig," he says and shakes my hand.

He's not flattered.

"I saw you last night at Fiddlestix" He says.

"Oh wow, really? That's so funny because I'm not even 21 and they let me in!

Isn't that funny?" I squealed.

"Great," he says as he gets a coffee refill.

"Well, nice to meet you," I say and walk away.

I would like to add that I was wearing my Dirty Dancing jeans.

Craig was extremely good looking, but it was much more than that.

He was very sexy. In charge. Authoritative. Confident.

I must keep him from ever meeting Judy, I make a mental note.

He had a grown up job, an apartment, and a brand new truck.

I was extremely attracted to Craig. I loved the way he looked at me, the way he smelled, his smile.

Every day, I'd go into the dining hall for breakfast, lunch, and dinner. I'd be sure to stop by and see him at every meal.

Sometimes I had to go up and get seconds or thirds just to be able to casually say hello in a very nonchalant and ambiguous, non-desperate kind of way.

"Oh, hi, I forgot you work here, that's right," I'd say as I went up to get another grilled cheese.

Finally after several days of breakfast. Lunch. And Dinner.

I went into his office where he was catching up on some paperwork.

"Hi!" I say with a huge smile.

He's friendly but tells me he's really busy doing his paperwork.

"I can see that," I say as I sit down, smiling.

"I really am busy, but maybe we can get together sometime," he says.

"Well, let's see," I say as I opened my day timer. "I have Thursday night available, is that good for you, Thursday? Thursday evening?"

"Sure" he says, "I'll give you a call."

"Ok," I say, not budging from the chair until he asks for my phone number.

"Ok," well, see you later," He says.

"Don't you need my phone number, you know, to call me?" I say.

Then I added, "How can you call someone if you don't have their number?"

Craig called me and we ended up going on our first date.

I spent all day picking out the perfect outfit.

I went through every single piece of clothing in my closet and configured every possible combination for the perfect first date outfit.

I settled on a mock turtleneck long sleeved shirt, baggy jeans three sizes too big and my awesome white Converse High Tops.

Stellar hair and makeup.

I didn't want him to think I was slutty or easy. Or trying too hard. Especially because it was like pulling teeth getting him to ask me out it seemed.

We saw a movie, went out for dinner and then I gave him a tour of the NAU campus. It was sweet and romantic and perfect.

After our date I went straight to Judy's room.

I grabbed her family size package of Oreos and sat on her bed.

"Judy, I like him, I really like him..." I say scraping the cream out of the Oreos with my teeth and throwing away the actual cookie part.

"That's really gross," Judy says about my Oreo eating technique.

Did he kiss you?" she asks.

"Oh, yes," I said.

"Yes he did...it was...it was....magical," I said, and added "I didn't want the date to end."

Then I grew nervous.

"What if he doesn't call me? What if he didn't think our date was wonderful and perfect like I did?" I said as I shoved a cookie in my mouth.

"No, no, I'm sure he likes you and he'll call," Judy whispered like Marilyn Monroe as she took the remaining Oreos away from me.

He did call.

He called and we completely and utterly fell in love with each other.

We only saw each other twice a week, due to his busy work schedule.

Jon said this was probably a good thing due to my "unpredictable mood swings and tendency to obsess too much over guys I hardly know."

True.

That's the face I want to see every morning when I wake up for the rest of my life, I thought.

Craig went back home to Chicago for Christmas break, and I went to my parent's house in Phoenix, so we were apart for about a week.

When he came back to Flagstaff I had it in my head that this is too good to be true.

Maybe when he went back to Chicago he'd come to his senses and was going to dump me.

I started to believe this. I was worried. I was anxious.

I couldn't shake the feeling that it was going to end.

Please God, don't let this end.

Craig showed up at my door, on time as always.

"I have something for you," He said as he smiled.

"Is it a list of reasons why we're not compatible?" I say, as a close my eyes tight, bracing for his answer.

"No, silly," he said and gave me a perfect, gorgeous, dewy red rose.

No thorns.

I grinned from ear to ear, took the rose, threw it over my shoulder and hugged him really, really tight.

On our third or fourth date, we went to a house party up in Flagstaff.

This is when I knew I was really falling for him.

We were having some laughs and drinks.

Very low key.

Then I walked down the hallway to use the ladies' room, and saw people were smoking drugs.

I went back to the main room and sat down next to Craig with my arms crossed.

"Are you ok?" He asked, like a gentlemen.

"Yes, but I don't really want to stay too much longer, would you mind very much if we left?"

"Why, what's going on?"

"Well, some of the people here are smoking drugs and I don't like drugs," I said.

Then I added, "I honestly don't like drugs."

At this pivotal moment, I thought well, it was nice knowing you, and I expected to leave the party never hear from Craig again.

I expected him to laugh at me, call me a prude, or a square or tell me I'm lame.

That's not how things went down though.

Not at all.

He stood up and went up to the guy smoking the drugs and I'm not kidding this is what he said.

He confidently and discretely put his hand on the guy's shoulder and goes "Dude, you need to get rid of that, it's making my girlfriend uncomfortable."

I had a huge smile on my face.

And here's the best part.

The guy not only got rid of the drugs, but it was in his own house!

That's how large and in charge my boyfriend was.

He was a badass.

A total badass.

And he understood me.

Completely.

And he didn't ask annoying questions like "How come it takes you so long to get ready?" Or "Why are you suddenly in a bad mood, blah blah."

No, he just went with it.

He was The Man.

He got it.

He got that I smoked Marlboro Reds and drank vodka nearly every day, but if someone lights up a doobie, I suddenly turn into a Quaker.

I love him, I thought. I absolutely love him.

I brought Craig home to introduce him to my family.

My Mom really liked Craig as soon as she met him.

She said, "MaryJo, I need to see you for a minute in the other room."

I got up, shrugged and winked at Craig.

My Mother then says, "He is absolutely wonderful, don't let Jenny near him."

"Why, because she's prettier and has a better personality?"

Then I started to worry.

Well, I introduced Jon and Craig at dinner and all went fine.

Craig knew I was nervous about the meeting, so he very casually said to me as we were leaving Jon's place, "She's not my type, you are."

Then he hugged me and said, "I love a girl who can't cook, sleeps till noon and lets the laundry pile to the ceiling."

I was like "Thank you Jesus."

Another great thing about Craig is he didn't take me out on dates, he took me on adventures.

We rarely went out to eat, which was perfect, because I really tried hard to maintain my figure, so guys who were "foodies" never interested me.

And most of the time, the adventures were a surprise. He would simply tell me what time he'd pick me up, and hint at what I should wear.

Oh, and he always parked, and walked up to my door and knocked, like a gentleman.

Craig was refined. Cavalier. Polished.

He always opened every door for me.

He always walked closest to the curb.

I would sooner walk into a door than open one for myself if I'm in the presence of a man.

He restored my faith in chivalry.

Anyway before one of our dates, he told me to wear boots.

No problem.

I had gorgeous $300 Italian leather boots in Laredo Vanilla.

And my accessories included my pearl earrings.

Perfect.

He picks me up and was like, "Um, I told you to wear boots because we're going on a scenic hike."

And I said, "Oh, are we going outdoors again?"

Which I loved, because Craig loved it, but I wasn't quite used to the idea.

I just didn't think being outdoors was, you know, *natural.*

But now I was dating The Brawny Man.

Even Jon agreed. One time she held up a package of Brawny Paper Towels and goes "You are dating the Brawny Man!"

I did learn to love being outdoors and once a year I go camping just to be able to say I enjoy the woods and fresh air.

One time he said he was taking me to a nice restaurant and I suggested we stay in, rent a movie and get some makings for vodka tonics...our special drink.

He goes "Are you sure? I'm happy to take you any place you'd like to go."

And I was like "I just want to spend time with you, I don't need to go anywhere."

And then he joked about my being a "cheap date."

And I said "My upfront costs are low, it's the maintenance fee's that'll get you.

Then I winked and said, "You know, upkeep."

I ended up marrying this man, a prince and the man of my dreams.

"Remember that morning we met?" Craig says to me.

"Of course, I introduced myself to you," I replied.

"Right, but I almost met you the night before..." he says.

"Really? What do you mean?" I ask, perplexed.

"I saw you at Fiddlestix and asked who you were because I thought you were so hot," He said.

He went on saying "The guys I was with said your name was 'Mary,' so I said 'Hi, Mary," and you completely ignored me.

"Isn't that funny?" He added.

By our junior year in college, Jon left NAU and had the full time task of caring for her Mom, who fell ill.

I hadn't seen Jon for a while. She looked really tired.

She told me about the financial problems and the stress of being a teenager who has to support herself and her mother, not knowing if they could make rent each month and buy groceries.

Fighting back tears she said, "Life is so hard right now."

She let out a sigh adding, "And the worst part is I feel like I could lose my mom, she could die, Jo."

Jon fought back the tears with all her might.

I didn't know what to say.

It hurt me to see my wonderful, beautiful, kind-hearted friend in such turmoil.

I wanted to take her pain away. I would have given anything to be able to help her.

Then, suddenly, at a loss for reassuring words...I glanced at her bangs.

I meekly said "What's up with your hair?"

She made a face. It was kind of like when you're watching a really bad movie and something unexpected and outside the story line takes place.

 "Wait.....what?" she said.

I grabbed a spray bottle of water, spritzed her a few times and began styling.

Styling my little heart out. Teasing, spraying water, teasing, spraying. And teasing some more.

"There" I said. "Is that better, do you feel better now?"

"Yes, I guess so..."

Then she looked in the mirror and said, "Wow, nice!"

"Only you can make someone feel better with spit and a comb."

I feigned humility, shrugged it off and said, "It's no biggie."

"Remember you used to do the girls' makeup in the dorm on Friday nights?" Jon reminisced.

"Oh yeah, that was fun."

The girls loved it. They would line up outside our door. Jon had the clipboard with the appointments booked.

"Did you cleanse your skin?" Jon would ask.
Check.

"Are you wearing moisturizer"?
Check.

"Did you bring clean makeup brushes?"
Check.

"Ok," Jon said, "She will see you now."

Then I would beautify them with tons of black eyeliner, bronzy highlighter, pearly pink lip gloss and Aquanet hairspray.

It didn't matter how short their hair was or what kind of cut they had. I teased it up to the sky. The bigger the hair, the closer to God, I say.

Every single girl left my room looking like a showgirl from Branson, MO.

"You could've charged them and they would've paid," Jon said.

"Nope, the sparkle in their eyes gave me all the satisfaction I needed."

Life was good.

The phone call came as a surprise.

There was no hello, no cushioning, and no warning.

Just an announcement.

It was 1990. Craig and I had just gotten married.

Jon had begun dating Carl, who was Craig's oldest friend from college, as well as the Best Man at our wedding.

It was fabulous. Until that phone call came.

"I have to break up with Carl." Jon said, almost in tears.

"Why?"

"He gave me something," Jon said.

I feared the worst.

"He gave me a sweater." She said soberly.

"That's terrible," I replied.

Jon and I had an unspoken rule to agree with each other even before we knew the facts.

This rule also applied to people. If one of us didn't care for someone, then the other one automatically didn't.

Example: I recently ran into an old acquaintance from college. I called Jon and said "I ran into Priscilla Wigfield today at the mall."

Jon goes "Oh my gosh! Wow! How is she?"

And I said "She's kind of...rude."

And Jon goes, "I never liked her."

Anyway, Jon went on to explain why the sweater signified the beginning of the end of her relationship with Carl.

They had been seeing each other for a short while, but the two seemed to really hit it off.

Please keep in mind, that just one day before the deal-breaking sweater arrived, Jon and I mapped a seating chart for their wedding, hammered out a guest list, chose a location for her bridal shower, selected three very attractive drapery patterns for their future home, and Jon decided who would be her maid of honor: Me or her sister Paige.

Paige.

"I want my wedding to be perfect. My gown, bouquet, invitations, color palette, cake, favors, everything," she'd say.

"From your lips to Martha Stewart's ears," I'd put my hand up and promise.

Back to the sweater.

"It's a pretty sweater." Jon went on, "But I would never ever wear something like this. It's all pink and girly and feminine."

Now, keep in mind, fashion is extremely important to Jon. Clothes have meaning to her and speak volumes about a person including their values, convictions and personal belief system.

"And," she said in the most ominous tone I hadn't heard from her before,

"It has bows on it, so help me God. A sweater with bows."

"No," I gasped in horror, hitting the phone on my forehead trying to figure out what possessed Carl to make such a flagrant error in judgment.

Then the real rant began. Jon's voice grew almost squeaky. The pitch was high, the words came out fast. I tried to keep up.

"This sweater represents what Carl thinks of me. It's what he expects from me, it's how he sees me. I am not the girl he thinks I am."

If there's one thing Jon hates is when a guy gives her a gift that in no way reflects her true personality.

"It's like he wants to put me in this weird box, I am not that girl. I'm not his little pink princess.

She went on with a very philosophical, existential, almost fatalistic monologue about the sweater.

Truthfully, I think Jon was still smarting from the matching teddy bear sweatshirt "situation" circa 1987.

Most people break up over issues such as different socio-economic backgrounds, opposing political ideals or deeply held convictions about religious affiliations.

Jon knew it wouldn't work out between her and Carl because of a sweater.

I believe it's true. They were not meant to be. They never would have stayed together or been happy.

"I know this is completely off topic and probably not the right time to ask, but, is there any possibility I would want the sweater?" I asked.

"Sure, you can have it. It's either give it away, or burn it."

"Ok, send it, but how many bows does it have on it"

"It has like, three bows and a ribbon weaved through the top."

"Oh, what are the bows made of?" I asked.

"Ribbon material."

"Ok, so the bows are part of the ribbon weaved through or are they separate pieces?"

"They're separate pieces."

"What color pink is it, like powder pink or more of a Pepto Bismol pink?"

"It's kind of like ballet-slippers pink and the bows are kind of darker pink, not super dark, but darker than ballet slippers."

"Ok, got it, so I could wear it with jeans, or like a skirt?"

"Yeah, either would be fine...just don't wear it with khaki's or like, capri pants."

"I never wear capri pants. I feel like they make my legs look short," I said.

"Your body shape is better in longer pants that are straight leg or slightly flared."

And the conversation kind of evolved from there and Carl wasn't mentioned again.

Ever.

"If I don't like it, I will send it back to you and then you can burn it."

"Ok, that's totally fine." Jon said.

Times have changed, but Jon and I are still best friends.

We have grown up now and face all of the usual adult struggles:

Gas prices, kids, husbands, pets, career decisions, bank statements, car repairs.

"No, no! Do not put that in the toilet," was literally how Jon answered the phone once when I called her. She was talking to one of her children, of course.

Years ago, Jon and her husband, Monty arrived in Phoenix for Monty's brother's wedding.

I was selected to babysit her son. I was thrilled.

Shane was 18 months old.

I had no idea what to do with a baby. We were at the kitchen table.

I sat there. He sat there.

I felt his big cow eyes on me, clutching a stuffed animal and a sippy cup.

"How are you?" I asked, not expecting an answer but at a loss for what to say.

Blank stare.

"Are you hungry?" I asked as I opened the freezer. "I have Lean Cuisines and Diet Pepsi," I offered.

Blank stare.

Then I let him play with my vacuum cleaner for the next few hours. He was a happy little boy.

I was so filled with emotion, looking at this precious baby.

Whenever I feel bad about something I know I can always call my best friend and she will always make me feel better and we will have ourselves a good giggle.

The one thing I love about Jon is she just enjoys my humor and has never uttered the phrase to me,

"Stop making this about you."

Even when I clearly make things about me.

She just gets it.

Case in point.

Jon and I were enjoying some m&ms and diet Pepsi one sunny afternoon in our dorm.

And I said, you know, we are a little bit like this candy.

"How so?" she asked.

Well, it's like, if you ever notice, in the boy department, they either like you or me. No boys ever like BOTH of us.

Like m&m's. Plain or peanut.

"Oh right!" Jon said.

Then after a moment of pondering, I said "I like to think of myself as a peanut m&m, and you're a plain m&m.

Are you ok with that?

"Totally." Jon smiled.

**"If I could only have one food the rest of my life?
That's easy, Pez. Cherry flavored Pez."**

That's from the movie Stand by Me, which Jon and I saw
in the theater our freshman year in college.

The movie has special significance because it's about
kids who were friends from childhood.

Jon and I see each other occasionally, but mostly we go
on with our busy lives and sometimes weeks pass when
we don't have a chance to talk.

That never changes the bond, though. We always pick
right up where we left off.

We traded in our junk food for organic salads and fruit
smoothies, but on occasion we get on the phone, and
stay up half the night talking about our families, fashion,
our love and adoration of Jesus, boys (the ones we
married) and what the future might hold.

And now Jon's Mom will text us "Girls! Go to sleep!"
which always makes us laugh.

And we still laugh so hard that our tummies ache.

Jon and I always say the best way to sum up our
friendship is from the last line in Stand by Me,

"I never had any friends later on like the friends I had
when I was twelve, does anyone?"

***

After Jon read this book, she liked it so much she told me I should write a sequel and I was like "Really?" and she goes, "Yeah, totally, you should totally write a sequel and I was like "Ok!"

So coming soon:

Primp Queen Career Girls
We'll have the Business Women's Special

Including the popular short Stories:

"Who Wants to Know Who Peggy Is?"

And the spellbinding sequel

"I'm Going to Say that I'm Peggy"

www.ingramcontent.com/pod-product-compliance
Lightning Source LLC
Chambersburg PA
CBHW072011040426
42447CB00009B/1582